**Community Care
Practice Handbooks**

*General Editor:* Martin Davie

# An Introduction to Social Work Theory

# Community Care Practice Handbooks

## *General Editor:* Martin Davies

# An Introduction to Social Work Theory

## Making Sense in Practice

**David Howe**

ASHGATE

First published by Wildwood House Limited
This edition reprinted 1992 by Arena

Published by
Ashgate Publishing Limited
Gower House
Croft Road
Aldershot
Hants GU11 3HR
England

Ashgate Publishing Company
Suite 420
101 Cherry Street
Burlington VT 05401-4405
USA

Ashgate website: http://www.ashgate.com

Reprinted 1993, 1994, 1996, 1998, 2000 (twice), 2002 , 2003

CIP catalogue record for this book are available from the
British Library and the US Library of Congress

ISBN 1 85742 138 8

Printed and bound in Great Britain by Athenaeum Press Ltd,
Gateshead, Tyne & Wear

# Contents

# Permissions

The author and publishers would like to thank a number of publishers for their kind permission to reproduce extracts from the following: *Feminist Social Work with a Women's Group* by Arnon Donnelly (University of East Anglia, Social Work Monographs, 1986); *Social Work as Art* by Hugh England (Allen and Unwin, 1986); *Behavioural Treatment of Problem Children* by Martin Herbert (Academic Press, 1981); 'Psychodynamic Approach to Casework' by Joan Hutten (*Social Work Today*, 24 February 1972); *Helping in Social Work* by Bill Jordan (Routledge and Kegan Paul, 1979); 'Bringing Up Baby' by Paul Vevers (*Community Care*, 1981); 'A Framework for Theory in Social Work' by Colin Whittington and Ray Holland (*Issues in Social Work Education*, vol.5, no.1, 1985, A.T.S.W.E.); *Social Work with Undervalued Groups* by Ruth Wilkes (Tavistock Publications, 1981).

# Acknowledgements

The framework that supports the body of this book was first constructed in 1980 in the wake of major developments in the world of social theory. In particular, I owe a considerable debt to the work of Gibson Burrell and Gareth Morgan (1979). I have adopted their analysis of social theory and used it to organize my own thinking about social work and its theories. Several generations of social work students at the University of East Anglia have been presented with versions of the material contained in this book. Their reactions have helped refine my ideas and their organization.

Anne Borrett typed the manuscript with such speed and accuracy that I managed to keep all my deadlines. I am most grateful to her.

D.H.

# Introduction

When, not for the first time, I found myself saying to a student social worker that there is more than one way to skin a cat, I realized that there was much to be said about different ways of explaining the world.

Many social workers, when thinking about their work, seem to have difficulty in seeing problems from more than one point of view. The advantage of this broader viewpoint is that people, problems and situations look different as the angle of understanding changes. Potentially feasible actions shift as the perspective is altered. The world becomes a more fluid place; it also looks altogether more interesting. Thus it is necessary to consider the nature of theory, provided theory is something to do with the way we try to make sense of the objects we see and the people we meet. Different theories allow us to set about problems in varying ways.

The mention of theory and skinning of cats does not, however, bring about instant joy in the hearts of many social workers. For them, the relationship between theory and their practice remains something of a mystery. Some fret over it, searching for an answer. Others resolve the mystery by saying that there is no mystery, that their practice is not related to any theory. They say such things as 'I practise intuitively' or 'a commonsense approach suits me'.

Knowing no theory and having even less to do with it is taken as a sign of practical virtue, a down-to-earth wisdom that has learned how to deal with the pretensions of effete theoreticians. There is something smug about those who describe themselves as practical-folk, people who don't go in for airy-fairy notions. Talk of theory, they say, no doubt is clever stuff, but with the clear implication that they can well manage without it thank-you-very-much — and if they have no need of it, then there is no need for it.

This book will show that it is not so easy to dismiss theory. In fact, it will be argued that not only is theory in social work unavoidably integral to any practice, but also its relegation to an implicit, un-articulated status leads to a poor, indeed dishonest practice. In making this argument, this book acts as an informed and wide-ranging guide to social work and its major theories.

The clients of social workers have a number of interesting points to make on these matters, and it is this group of people that are first highlighted. As will be seen, they make two important observations.

Firstly, they prefer social workers who know where they are with their clients. Secondly, as clients, they like to know where they are with their worker. Being able to describe and define the situation is aided by an understanding of theory.

# 1 The Consumer Reports

It was not until the late 1960s that researchers thought to ask clients what they felt about social workers and the service that they gave. As well as satisfying social work's curiosity, it was recognized that the provision of an 'effective service requires us to know something about the responses and reactions of those we seek to help' (Sainsbury 1975, p.1). More broadly, the pursuit of the consumer's view was part of a general movement in the social sciences away from simply seeing people as objects in society to understanding them as individuals who have personal views of the world. .

In social work, the consumer's view is not just an interesting aside. If social work is to be a personal social service then it becomes necessary to know how the service is being personally experienced. The client's perception is an integral part of the practice of social work. It was recognized that it was important to know what consumers felt and understood to be happening if social work was to be appropriate and effective. For both researchers and practitioners this opened up an entirely different line of practice. Explanations, values and methods changed. The view of the other was sought and the client spoke.

**What clients say**
Davies (1985, p.26), in his review of the literature on the client's perspective, identifies two aspects of practice that consumers feel social workers should get right: the quality of the relationship; and the achievement of results. Clients do not like social workers who are cool, detached, career-minded or suggest that they are just doing their job. In Sainsbury's (1975) study, Mrs Underwood said:

> It's got to be done on a friendly basis with me. It's no good them coming and just sitting and listening to you and not caring a damn (p.89).

Clients do like workers who show friendliness, homely qualities and honesty. 'I just felt like I was talking to an old friend,' says Mrs Mole in *The Client Speaks* (Mayer and Timms 1970, p.82), 'and just pouring out my troubles.'

Closely bound up with the worker's style and the satisfactory achievement of results is the issue of the client knowing where he or she is with the social worker. The need to understand why the worker is involved and what is going on runs through all the consumer reports.

Ideally, the worker should be clear and explicit both about her purpose and method of working.

Many clients felt confused, baffled and even irritated by social workers who were vague or unclear about their intentions. 'An uneasy lack of clarity' about why social workers visited troubled many of Sainsbury's respondents (Sainsbury 1980). Clients new to the personal social services often have no precise knowledge of what social workers do. Mr Zebedee in Rees's study (1978, p.75) recalled his social worker's first visit, 'he just nosed around in here, took particulars, just like the police when they come in to see who done the meter'. Rees (p.75) goes on to observe that, by making enquiries beyond first meetings, social workers gave an impression of being interested, 'yet, subsequently, they felt reluctant to take further initiatives and withdrew without any explicit agreement'. Thus, clients were left hazy about the purpose of the worker's visit, as in the case of Mrs May:

> I wondered why he was coming. He seems to think I'm going to take another dose of pills. When he comes it's embarrassing because he doesn't seem to know what to say (Rees 1978, p.99).

Ambiguities over intervention and clashes in perspective also became a source of client dissatisfaction. In Mayer and Timms's (1970) investigations, many clients remained unaware that the worker's psychoanalytic outlook accounted for the interest being shown in their past and the family's relationship in the present:

> When we came out of there the fourth time, my husband said, 'what do you think of it?' and I said, 'I don't know what to think of it'. Then my husband said, 'He just don't give you any idea what he's going to do or anything. He just keeps on saying come back and have some more talks and he says he's going to have more talks and more talks. Well, while he's doing that, we're not getting anywhere. Penny's the problem, not us' (ibid., p.71).

In similar vein, Rees (1978, p.101) cites the case of the social worker who was seen by the family as coming to collect the rent but he himself regarded this as an opportunity to discuss the possibility of the father getting a job and check the welfare of the children whom he suspected of being maltreated. Similarly, a women who had sought to adopt a child found some of her experience with social workers 'extremely unsatisfactory', she told Timms (1973, p.6), 'because they never explained procedures to us so we never knew what the next stage would be or how many hurdles lay in front of us'.

Clients who understand the worker's role and appreciate their methods of working appear more satisfied. When explanations are made clear and explicit, the client's confusion and anger disappear. Corby (1982, p.630) records that clients prefer social workers who are 'straight', who let them know where they stand. A general sense of progress that the involvement was leading somewhere recognizable was viewed favourably. Indeed, a certain amount of 'acceptable directiveness' (Sainsbury 1975, p.80) was felt to aid the worker's relationship with the client. The subsequent experiences of the woman seeking to adopt with another agency confirm the value of practising in a clear and open way. 'The meeting . . . gave the social worker a chance to explain exactly how their adoption procedure worked and this was most helpful as we then knew where we were throughout the negotiations' (Timms 1973, p.19).

### Effective practice

What clients say is matched by what observers see to be effective in practice. Fischer (1978, pp.222–3), in a comprehensive review of the literature, concludes that, in order to be effective, workers must succeed in the two following areas:

1    They must create those personal conditions which establish a relationship of trust, caring and acceptance, thereby increasing the client's amenability to therapeutic influence. It appears, therefore, that the quality of the relationship is important in social work practice. Social workers should be 'responsive'.
2    They must employ clear and explicit procedures. The purpose of the worker's involvement must be understood by the worker and the client. Good practitioners make deliberate use of well articulated theories and methods which organize, order and direct practice in a way that is recognized by both worker and client. Social workers should be 'systematic'.

Failure in one or both of these areas leads to weak practice. Truax and Carkhuff (1967) were amongst the first to identify the value of empathy, genuineness and warmth in successful therapeutic relationships. The absence of any of these 'core conditions' did not equate with satisfactory outcomes.

Mayer and Timms (1970, p.144), reflecting on the insight-oriented techniques of their family welfare workers, felt that 'an approach of this type, our data strongly suggest, will prove ineffective unless clients first acquire some understanding of the assumptions underlying its use'. Sainsbury (1975, p.83) reminds social workers of their responsibility for shaping the content of the interview and quotes Mrs Price, one of his respondents, on the characteristics she prefers in a social worker, 'they've got to be strong. They should be able to take control of the situation'.

Social workers who are able to state what it is they think is going on and how things should be tackled are appreciated by clients. Yet the evidence is that many practitioners are weak in these critical respects. Corby (1982, p.627), for example, in his examination of long-term practice, found that social workers were clear about their description and assessment of cases but uncertain about what it was they were trying to achieve. When clients themselves were asked what they thought their social workers were trying to do to help them 'many were unaware of the idea of any strategy on the part of the social workers' (Corby, p.628).

Rees (1978, p.43), too, records that some of his respondents could not state the objectives in their work, or, if they did, they were couched in very general terms such as 'to make people happier'. In fact, means and ends often became confused. 'He requires the kind of help that might come from building up a relationship', believed one worker (ibid., p.44). Throughout most of the consumer studies, social workers were clear about the value of a good relationship but muddled about the actual purpose of their involvement. This left clients bemused.

## The structure of practice

The relationship and the use of interpersonal skills has received a good deal of attention in social work practice over recent years. Although the use of direction and order by the worker is a recognized part of skilled practice, the characteristics of sequentially organized work have been examined less rigorously. This book looks at the nature of a structured practice – the process of social work – and considers its relationship to social work theory.

Both social workers and clients should know where they are and where they would like to go. If you do not know where you are, you will not know in which direction to move. If you do not know where you are going, you will not know when you have arrived. Drift and a lack of purpose in much social work practice suggests many social workers have little idea of place in their work with clients. Thus, a sense of location and a sense of direction should structure practice. With her client, the worker should be clear about her role, purpose and methods of working. What has brought them together and the expectations each has of the other should be discussed and made mutually clear. These are the ingredients of good practice. This is the language of organization, order and structure. It dispels confusion and prevents talk which is at cross-purposes.

During the 1970s the basic pattern of a structured practice was formulated (Goldstein 1973, Siporin 1975, Pincus and Minahan 1973). In some hands it became known as the social work process (Butrym 1976, p.81). In this, the worker is required to think and act systematically. With the client, the worker needs to be clear who she is and why she is there. Nothing should be assumed. What may be a daily and accustomed way of thinking to the social worker is an entirely new experience for the client.

According to Fischer (1978, p.138), the most crucial aspect of structure is planning. This involves making a careful assessment, formulating goals, developing programmes and sequenced steps, choosing methods and establishing criteria against which the outcome can be judged. At the very outset, the client has to be involved in what is going on, aware of what is being done and why. Clients who remain unclear about the purpose and methods of social work practice tend to drop out (Briar 1966). The worker should be clear not only about her position, but should actively discover the client's expectations of the involvement. Out of this demand for clarity and the avoidance of 'double-agendas' arose the widespread use of the 'contract' — sometimes written, often spoken. The contract is usually specific, spelling out in concrete detail what each party will do and expect. As Fischer (1978, p.142) argues, 'contracts foster explicitness, clarity and openness in the relationship between worker and client. They also provide a built-in framework for establishing reciprocal accountability.'

This brief survey of the client's view suggests that social workers should be able to answer the following five questions if they are to establish a practice that is clear, organized and structured:

| | | |
|---|---|---|
| 1 | What is the matter? | The worker needs to recognize and identify the problem. |
| 2 | What is going on? | The situation has to be assessed, interpreted and explained. |
| 3 | What is to be done? | In the light of the assessment, the social worker and client decide on their goals, making plans and clarifying intentions. |
| 4 | How is it to be done? | The methods by which the goals are to be achieved have to be chosen. |
| 5 | Has it been done? | The outcome is evaluated. |

The views of clients and the observations of researchers leave no room for complacency on the part of social workers. The questions need to be asked with persistence. Answers should be sought with insistence by workers, clients and supervisors alike. But there is one more thing to note. Although the answers to each of the five questions may be given loudly and clearly from individual social workers, each social worker may give a *different* answer in the *same* situation. This curious state of affairs takes us into the world of theory.

# 2 Making Sense

## Seeing and understanding

For different people, the world around just looks different — physically, psychologically and socially. Ways of viewing the world and explaining how objects, people and situations work is the province of theory. In this way competing theories lead to contrasting explanations of the same phenomena.

For example, in geology, the historical reason for the existence of great mountain chains has received two contrasting explanations. The first theory suggested that the earth is gradually cooling down. As it cools, the planet shrinks and like an apple that dries and shrivels or a balloon that deflates and wrinkles, its surface begins to crumple and fold and this we see as mountains. The other theory takes a directly opposite view. The earth's core and mantle actually generate heat through radioactive decay. This heat wells up towards the surface, and like porridge in a pan, it crumples, fractures and disturbs the crust. As pieces or 'plates' of crust glide over the surface, some collide and are pushed into huge mountainous blocks. Each theory of mountain building understands the same geological condition in a fundamentally different way. The accounts are mutually exclusive.

Similarly, in the case of mental disorder, theoretical disputes have led to varying and conflicting explanations. Moreover, these different understandings have led to different practices and treatments. If the cause of madness is said to be the possession of the individual by evil spirits, the appropriate response is exorcism. When the explanation of mental disturbance lies with chemical imbalances in the brain, treatment by drugs is recommended. If mental confusion is generated in the disturbed communication patterns of family life, family therapy is offered. What is to be done depends on what it is you think is going on.

So, returning to the relationship between good practice and the structure of social work, it is now possible to sense that the content of good practice is highly contested ground. The problems seen, the assessments made, the goals set and the methods employed vary according to the theoretical position held. But although the need for clear structure and order in social work practice has been strongly argued and fully articulated, the theories that underpin it have not received such a close examination, at least as they impinge on the shape and direction of practice. In some quarters there has been what

Hardiker and Barker (1981, p.2) call an 'anti-intellectual stance' in which the role of theory is avoided. We all have ideas about the way things are and views about what should be done. Each way of making sense of what is going on amounts to having a theory. Of course, my understanding of the situation may not be the same as yours. Nevertheless, it is reasonable to ask of me, particularly in a morally and socially fraught area such as welfare work, how I am seeing events, what I understand to be happening and what actions I propose to take.

The rest of this book examines the characteristics of different social work theories. It seeks to explore how the identification of problems, the setting of goals and the choice of methods depends on how people and their situation are being explained and so lead to different kinds of practice. So, although the social worker may well know where she is and where she is going, which from the client's point of view is good, the starting point and destination vary depending on the initial outlook. By understanding how theory determines the 'process' of practice, I hope to show that there are many possible starting points and numerous places to go. To travel at all is to hold ideas about the behavioural and social terrain over which we journey. To show no interest in social work theory is simply to travel blind. This is bad for practice and unhelpful to clients.

However, before proceeding any further, a little more groundwork is needed. It is important to say something about the nature and purpose of theory in general. More particularly, it is necessary to look at social and behavioural theories and consider the special problems that they pose. As social work theories derive largely from psychology and sociology, but apply themselves to people who have problems and people who are problems, the special characteristics of these occupational theories will be considered.

## Theory

When people encounter physical objects or other human beings, they attempt to make sense of them, account for their characteristics and general behaviour. Ideas are generated about 'what is going on' and 'why things are as they are and do what they do'. Feeling uncertain about the way the material or social world is liable to behave is disconcerting. We seek to reduce such uncertainty by having ideas or theories about the people and objects around us, making them more intelligible and less prone to act in ways that surprise, upset or threaten. We look for patterns and regularities. We could not cope with a chaotic, random universe where events just happen for no apparent reason. In a world where there are no rules, no rhythms and no knowing where we are from one moment to the next, life would be impossible.

We try to recognize these patterns, indeed we actively create them. Simply to describe what we see requires some mechanism by which to organize our perceptions. Most of us describe situations with reference to some preconceived notion of the possible order of things. It is very difficult to view events with complete naïveté. We are disposed to see the world in a familiar light. Butrym (1976) quotes Kline in similar vein:

> We should regard any theory about physical space as a purely subjective construction and not impute to it any objective reality. Man constructs a geometry, Euclidean or non-Euclidean, and decides to view space in those terms. The advantage of doing so, even though he cannot be sure space possesses any of the characteristics of the structure he has built up in his own mind, are that he can think about space and nature and use his theory in scientific work (p.67).

Models, acting as analogies, can also be used to order, define and describe phenomena. They do not explain the things seen, but they do begin to impose some low level order on what is otherwise a jumble of information. Models act as bricks in theory-building (Hardiker and Barker 1981, p.21). Evans (1976) gives an example:

> A model of the British class structure may describe the elements in it without necessarily explaining the relationship between these elements or the social processes which are necessary to sustain or change them. A theory on the other hand attempts to go beyond simple description to (often causal) explanation (p.180).

Theories are not absolute notions of the way things really are, but, so long as they account for what appears to be happening in a way that satisfies the observer, they are retained. Theories provide 'workable definitions' of the world about us. They make it intelligible. In a very real way, theory-building is reality-building (Argyris and Schon 1974, p.18). Our theories define what we see.

Closely tied to the need to understand and explain is the wish to predict. Knowing what will happen next, and calculating the effect if certain things are done, altered or introduced, is necessary if the world is not only to make sense but to become available for the practical purposes of men and women. Explanations imply predictions and predictions are crucial if people and things are to be manufactured and manipulated, changed and controlled in a reliable way. So having a theory about the cause of a disease such as smallpox, and understanding the way the body creates antibodies to combat infective organisms, allowed Edward Jenner in 1798 to inoculate human beings with the relatively harmless virus of cowpox or 'vaccinia'. The body was stimulated to produce large numbers of the appropriate antibodies giving lasting protection against smallpox.

Theories are products of the time in which they were formulated. Most theories are short-lived. When a theory fails to account adequately for things or too many exceptions occur to the predicted state of affairs, that theory is no longer doing its job. Uncertainty returns. Control is lost. Better explanatory schema are sought. This often occurs when the objects of interest are observed in greater detail and more and more is found out about them. Facts no longer fit together in the way they should, things no longer quite add up, anomalies appear. The search is then on for a theory that is more successful in solving these problems that the practitioners and operators in that field recognize as acute (Kuhn 1970, p.23). Lord Macaulay wrote:

> Experience can never be divided or even appear to be divided, except with reference to some hypothesis. When we say that one fact is inconsistent with another fact, we mean only that it is inconsistent with *the theory* which we have founded on that fact. But if the fact be certain, the unavoidable conclusion is that our theory is false (Macaulay 1889, p.162).

For example, early Western medicine had the idea that a person's appearance, personality and temperament were determined by the relative presence of each of the four body fluids or 'cardinal humours': blood, phlegm, choler and melancholy. According to these early theorists, emotional equilibrium and general health depended on an appropriate balance amongst these four humours. Imbalances resulted in illness or emotional disturbance. People were described as sanguine, phlegmatic or prone to melancholy. Thus, those who were ill, disturbed or in 'bad humour' as a result of, say, having too much of the fluid 'blood' were bled in order for the humours to recover their equilibrium. However, this simple account of physiological and psychological functioning could not cope with growing information about the body and its processes. Nor could it suggest reliable treatments. Over the last four centuries these primitive concepts of body chemistry have been replaced by more subtle and complex theories of biochemistry, which provide comprehensive sets of explanation and allow more efficacious treatments.

It will now be apparent that one of the functions that 'a theory should serve is that of preventing the observer from being dazzled by the full blown complexity of natural and concrete events. The theory is a set of blinders' permitting the observer to go about abstracting from nature's complexity in a systematic and manageable manner (Hall and Lindzey 1957). 'The flux of experience is continuous and has no structure of its own. It is we who impose shape upon it to make of it a world to live in' (Cupitt 1985, p.20).

So, although phenomena are in themselves meaningless, meaning is imposed in order to render the world intelligible, manageable and usable. The realization that people create order and sense, rather than discover it, first came to Kant from his great critical examination of knowledge. 'In pre-critical philosophy people believed in an objective intelligible order, to which the human mind sought to accommodate itself' (ibid., p.247). The meaning of things was outside the minds of people; it lay 'out there' in the objective condition of the things themselves. Kant reversed this outlook. 'His enquiry into the process by which the human mind converts raw and formless experience into ordered objective knowledge had led him to a revolutionary change of viewpoint' (ibid., p.247). More formally, a theory may now be defined as a set of concepts and propositions that present an organized view of phenomena. By proposing order and pointing out relationships, theories enable their users to do four important things as they set about their particular bit of the world:

1 To describe.
2 To explain.
3 To predict.
4 To control and bring about.

Clearly, social workers are people who attempt to do all four of these things. In their work for courts and case conferences, they are expected to describe and explain the present behaviour and anticipate the future conduct of their clients. Policemen, relatives and neighbours expect social workers 'to do something about' delinquent adolescents and neglectful parents, to mend broken marriages and cure disturbed children. However, when people, and not just objects and their properties, become the subject to be explained, predicted and changed, the type of theory used, in fact its very nature, becomes highly problematic.

## Behavioural and social theory

The need for explanations results from the discovery of problems and from the deliberate puzzling over the nature of things. Scientific theories offer formalized approaches to making sense of the objects about us. They may be termed systematic theories: general ideas formulated for a purpose.

In general, the utility of theory in modern science is to summarize existing knowledge, to categorize and relate observations, and to predict the occurrence of as yet unobserved events and relationships on the basis of the explanatory principles embodied in the theory. So, for example, ideas about a force, known as gravity, exerted by massive bodies, allowed astronomers to describe and explain the exact movement of the planets around the sun. It also enabled them to predict the presence of a ninth, as yet undiscovered planet, which was necessary in order to make sense within terms of gravitational theory, of the complete movement of the already known planets. In 1930 the missing planet was duly discovered at the darkest, deepest edges of the solar system and was aptly named Pluto.

Life, however, is not quite so straightforward for the behavioural and social theorist. As well as being observers, men and women are also the objects of observation. However, unlike most natural objects, the men and women under observation also have ideas about what is going on. This introduces a new and very fluid dimension to the study of people and their society. Cohen (1968) describes the problem in this way:

> By participating in social life men have a far greater chance of comprehending certain features of its fundamental reality than they do by participating in the natural world. The fact that men are physical objects does not give them access to the nature of matter or life. The fact that men are social subjects, as well as objects, does give them an opportunity to gain some idea of the nature of social relationships and of the wider context of these. For social reality does not have mechanisms which are *necessarily* hidden from the observation of all those who participate in it.
>
> The second reason, which is related to the first, is that in participating in social life men are *encouraged* to form certain ideas about its reality. Of course the same is true of their participation in the natural world: to control and forecast natural events, men must have ideas about their nature. But there is a difference. Men do not, for the most part, create either the natural world or its mechanisms. They *do* create their social world, even if, for the most part, they do so unwittingly. But, in so far as their actions and interactions are responsible for the creation of the social world in which they participate, men may be encouraged by their situations to comprehend these fundamental realities to the best of their abilities.
>
> The third reason, which is related to the other two, concerns the nature of social reality itself. Whereas men may be right to assume that the nature of physical reality is independent of their ideas of it, they would be wrong to assume this of much of social reality . . .
>
> The most fundamental idea concerning the nature of social reality is that the properties of the elements of social phenomena obtain many of their characteristics from the larger phenomena of which they are a part, while the larger entities obtain their characteristics mostly from the relations between the parts of which they are composed. This difficult paradox has been the source of much irritation to social theorists (p.10).

Men and women, therefore, can never simply be 'objects' of study.

They have subjective views about their own, and other people's, situation. It is the individual's subjective understanding of what is going on which is every bit as important to the social theorist as the external characteristics and behaviours that others may observe. This state of affairs generates fundamental issues in the study of psychology and sociology. What is the nature of the phenomena under study (you, me and other people)? How is sense made of what is seen? What are the methods to be used to gain relevant information? What information is to be counted as relevant? These are important but difficult questions to answer. In so far as social workers derive much of their working knowledge from behavioural and social theories, they face similar conceptual and methodological problems. On what basis are we making sense of this person and his situation? What things do we need to know in order to explain what is happening? How do we discover and 'get at' this knowledge? What sort of things can we do or say in order to bring about a calculated change? Thinking along these lines, Whittaker (1974) believes that it is essential for social workers to have some understanding of the theories that underlie their practice:

> This is not only because it is from theory that strategies of treatment are derived, but also because implicit in each theory is a value orientation and view of man which may have a profound effect on the nature of the helping service delivered by the professional (p.62).

## Social work theory

All occupational and activity groups wish to know as much as they can about the things with which they deal. They want to understand their bit of the world. This allows them to cope better with the situations in which they find themselves and generally be more successful in their purposes. Each group is interested in certain types of phenomena and assembles a particular range of theories which might say something useful about their subject of interest. In this sense, knowledge is socially distributed. Butrym (1976) believes that:

> Social workers can no more afford to avoid making and using generalisations than any other group of people who seriously intend to improve the quality of their service by both learning from the experience and the mistakes of their predecessors and offering their own accumulated understanding for use by their successors (p.67).

The bit of the world in which social workers are interested is people — people who are in distress or people who are a cause of distress. Now this is a particularly complex area in which to become involved. Feelings tend to run high and points of view clash. As they try to get to grips with the consequences of poverty or cope with disturbed children, social workers seek explanations, they want to know what makes people 'tick' and why there is deprivation amidst plenty. Social workers say and do certain things and ponder their effects on other people. They practise particular actions and techniques in the hope that they have a predictable effect upon the behaviour and conditions of their clients.

To do their job well, social workers want to know what is going on and, once they find themselves in that position, they are in the realms of theory. They are looking for patterns and pathways through the flux of events that besiege and confuse them. Theories help guide our behaviour. 'The function of knowledge in social work,' writes Polansky (quoted in Siporin 1975, p.102), 'is to increase the practitioner's ability to exercise conscious and deliberate mastery over his environment.'

For example, in attempting to help old people with their personal care and housing needs, social workers may understand their problem in a number of ways. A daughter's refusal to help support her increasingly fragile father may have something to do with her fear of handling someone who is growing more dependent and messy. The guilt and anger that this produces causes both daughter and father problems over and above his fragile condition. Or, the inability of an otherwise fit and healthy septuagenarian to cook and clean for himself after the recent death of his wife may be seen as the final outcome of an unequal society in which women domestically serve men. Elsewhere, the low priority given by the Housing Department to the provision of sheltered accommodation may mean the reluctant removal of the old person to a residential home. Depending on the interpretation, the social worker could find herself providing psychodynamic casework to the daughter, mobilizing community support alongside training an old man for independent living, or initiating a long-term political campaign to encourage the Housing Committee to reassess its policy on meeting the needs of old people. The understanding reached is not self-evidently present in the problem itself. What is seen and done will depend upon the explanatory framework held. Shift the framework and its grid of understanding and the situation is perceived anew.

For many social workers, the mere mention of 'theory' leaves them cold. They say they never use it or doubt its relevance. In Stevenson and Parsloe's (1978, pp.133—5) study of local authority fieldworkers, many of those interviewed felt 'ambivalent' about discussing their work in theoretical terms. It was rare for social workers to incorporate theory into descriptions of their practice. Several said they were unaccustomed to conceptualizing or reflecting about their work:

> If you asked me to state a theory here and now, I wouldn't have a clue but my thinking and approach have been formed by them.
>
> I often feel that I'm acting far more from instinct than from knowledge really or skills . . . I'm working very intuitively sometimes (ibid.).

Stevenson and Parsloe conclude that, 'on the whole', our respondents' description of their work with clients did not suggest that practice was drawn from specific theoretical perspectives (p.134).

Can social workers simply say they do not need or use theory, and rest self-satisfied on intuition and commonsense? Briar and Millar (1971) do not think that they can:

> The choice for the practitioner is not whether to have a theory but what theoretical assumptions to hold. All persons acquire assumptions or views on the basis of which they construe and interpret events and behaviour, including their own. These assumptions frequently are not explicit but are more what has been called 'implicit theories of the personality'. Thus, the appeal for practitioners to be atheoretical amounts simply to an argument that theory ought to be implicit and hidden, not explicit and self conscious . . . Whether implicit or explicit, the social worker's particular assumption about human behaviour can be expected to influence his professional actions and, therefore, have important consequences for his clients (pp.53–4).

Similar distinctions between explicit and implicit use of theory have echoed through the social work literature. For example, Siporin (1975, pp.94–5) believes that social workers need to have a *foundation knowledge* which consists of personality theory, social theory and social policy theory. These are theories about the person in society, about the relationship between the personality and the social world. Social work practice theory on the other hand:

> Is concerned with planned intervention and change activities in regard to personality and social systems. It deals with what social workers do in interacting with and helping clients and citizens with their social problems (ibid., p.95).

A widely quoted article by Evans (1976) also gives an account of how different 'types' of theory might be present in practice. He notes that there is a distinction between the scientific and experiential bases of social work. However, Evans also believes that it is inappropriate to think of this distinction as simply one between theory and experience:

> It also involves a distinction between explicit and implicit theory. I have already referred to the former as 'the theory of practice'; that theory which is derived from the social science knowledge base of social work. It may be useful to refer to the latter as 'practice theory'; that which is implicit in what social workers do and in how they make sense of their experience . . . Practice theories then are the 'commonsense' or 'homemade' theories which social workers carry around in their heads and which are implicit in their day-to-day activities (ibid., p.179).

This tempting formula, which identifies a 'theory of practice' and a 'practice theory', may prove to be more seductive than actually helpful. Hearn (1982) also takes Evans to task. He sees the distinction guilty of championing practice and in effect encouraging social workers to neglect more formal thoughts about social and behavioural theory. If the distinction is maintained, we are dangerously close to confirming *ad hoc* commonsense as acceptable occupational theory. This simply maintains the confusion that befuddles clients and social workers alike. It sustains the claim that theoretical ignorance is a professional virtue. It is not a virtue. It is an excuse for sloppy practice and technical dishonesty.

Corby's (1982) study of social workers in a long-term team reveals the vagueness that arises when workers just 'do' social work. He reports that 'most social workers found it difficult to explain how they were tackling problems' (ibid., p.626). Although they had a great deal of knowledge about their cases, in the main they remained descriptive and did not lead to definite strategies or clear means. He concludes that 'There were very few attempts to bring cases to successful conclusions. These findings are the logical outcome of an approach which does not set goals in the first place' (ibid., p.634).

If drift and purposelessness are to be avoided, practice needs to be set within a clear framework of explanation, the nature of which leads to a well articulated practice. As we have seen, there are a number of explanatory bases on which we can place ourselves. Each provides a platform from which contrasting courses of action may follow. It is the case, then, that 'reality . . . is not a hard, immutable thing, but is fragile . . . a thing to be debated, compromised and legislated' (McCall and Simmons 1966, p.42). Nevertheless the debate has to be out in the open. We need to declare our position so that others, particularly those with whom we work, can see what we are about and where we want to take them. If we approach people imaginatively, 'if we can use our theories to find out about the world, then our range of effective action increases, we become more free' (Craib 1984, p.10).

# 3 Sorting Out Social Work Theories

**Taking stock**

If your work is about people and their problems, one area of knowledge to which you are bound to turn is that produced by sociologists and psychologists. However, the status and variety of their knowledge can be quite bewildering. The temptation is simply to ignore it, though the case has already been made that this amounts to running blind in a field which already has more than enough boulders to trip, bruise and maim the unwary.

Even so, if the knowledge base appears tangled, it only adds to the difficulties experienced by the hard-pressed practitioner as she attempts to hack her way through the business of each day. The task, then, is to unravel and order the ideas that underpin the welter of social work theories, derived, as they are, from sociology and psychology. If practitioners are clear about where different theories lead them, they can plot their course of action with foresight and eyes wide open.

Over the years, social workers have acquired more and more theories. The fashions that breeze through the social sciences eventually waft into social work's corner and invariably some practitioners pick them up. Bits of psychoanalytic and learning theory, *gestalt* therapy and transactional analysis, interactionism and Marxism have all settled in social work.

It has long been recognized that, as an occupational group, social workers are not very good at discarding old theories. They accumulate and litter training curricula, textbooks and professional practices. From time to time there is the call to have a sort out, to tidy the place up a bit. At least this may remind us what we have by way of theoretical accommodation and what it is we think it covers. There has been an increasing sophistication in the ways social workers understand the need to get their theoretical house in order and the methods by which this might be done. The process has gone through seven stages: investigation; psychoanalysis; the diagnostic and functionalist schools; acquisition; taking an inventory; a common purpose and the unification of theory; and classifying social work theories.

*Investigation*　In their earliest days, around the turn of the century, social workers were 'doers' rather than 'thinkers'. Along with others, Mary Richmond spoke of social work as the 'art of helping'; the use of commonsense in uncommon situations (Goldstein 1973, p.26). The social worker was a collector of facts. She was an 'investigator'. In this first stage there was no explicit recognition or use of theory.

*Psychoanalysis*  The second stage marks the time when the only theory used by social workers was psychoanalytic theory. This represented a shift from the practical and material to the psychological and therapeutic. Social work in the 1920s and 1930s was said to have experienced a 'psychiatric deluge'. Although it has since been suggested that this heavy reliance on Freudian-based psychology reflected the interests of only a few élite psychiatric social workers, nevertheless, there was not much else around to dampen social work's theoretical spirits. With only one major intellectual base informing practice, the occupation's theoretical space remained simple and uncluttered.

*The diagnostic and functionalist schools*  By the 1930s, one of social work's treasured tenets had first seen the light of day. It came with the recognition that social workers should do it *with* clients and not *to* them. Jesse Taft and Virginia Robinson in the United States came under the influence of Otto Rank. They prodded social workers out of their Freudian passivity into a much more active relationship with the client. Help, they argued, did not come from tracking down and treating psychological maladies. Rather it was the experience of the helping relationship itself which led to a happy outcome.

Until the early 1950s, these two intellectual camps did battle. Each held different views about human nature and each offered help that was appropriate to their view of that nature. The diagnostic (Freudian) school was deterministic. The individual's behaviour was seen as the result of past causal events, particularly the experiences of early childhood. The client had to recognize the power of these formative years. Only insight into one's own psychological past could free one from the prison of present patterns of behaviour.

Adapting the ideas of Rank to the field of welfare produced the functionalist school of social work. Here, in contrast to Freudianism, the individual can be understood only in relation to his present circumstances. People are too complex to be diagnosed in relation to past events. On this basis, practice looks to the present, the 'here and now', the realities of the current situation which includes the function of the responding agency — hence the name, functionalist school. (This is not to be confused with 'functionalism' which is discussed in Chapters 4 and 5.) Reasoning along lines such as these meant that the relationship between the client and the social worker becomes an important experience in its own right. It is a vehicle that can be used to take the client, if he wishes, into more open, more realistic country. Goldstein (1973) offers a clear summary:

The Functionalist School . . . was based on a psychology of growth and a philosophy not unlike existentialism. Potentialities for change were not believed to be significantly determined by prior events. Given the opportunity, within a structured and socially productive relationship, the individual could work out his own changes. In the Diagnostic School, the center of change was in the social worker who diagnosed the problem, prescribed, and carried out a treatment plan. In the Functionalist School, the center of change was the client, while the social worker acted as helper and facilitator present within the relationship to enhance growth potential latent within the client (pp.38–9).

*Acquisition*  By the 1960s the elaboration of Freudian-based psychologies, the growth of learning theory and the increasing use of sociologically inspired ideas led to a huge increase in the number of theories available for application. This was a time of vigour. It was taken as a sign of health that social workers were chasing so many theoretical ideas. What was not recognized in the general enthusiasm was that the occupation's intellectual space was being rapidly but unsystematically filled. As the collectors brought home more theoretical trophies, the response was one of glee at the new prizes and not dismay at the untidiness of it all. This was the fourth phase, the stage of acquisition.

*Taking an inventory*  The fourth phase did not last for long. By the late 1960s there was a feeling that social workers should take stock. Making lists of the theories now in use was the thing to do in this, the fifth stage. Attempts were also made to assess the relative worth of each item, but essentially the exercise remained one of taking an inventory. This would produce a record of what theories the occupation now possessed. This was clearly the intention of Roberts and Nee (1970). They observed a proliferation of theoretical approaches to casework practice:

> These developments have been gradual and piecemeal and there have been few efforts to systematically compare the differences and similarities among the various approaches . . . Although it is desirable that theoretical knowledge grow through a cumulative process, there is also a need for periodic theoretical stock-taking and integration (ibid., p.xiv).

In their widely used compilation, Roberts and Nee record the presence of what, in 1969, were regarded as the most important theoretical items. Their list includes a variety of psychodynamically based approaches, behaviourist techniques, crisis intervention and the concept of socialization. The growing compass of social work thought and practice was said to indicate the intellectual well-being of the occupation. It also reflected the expanding horizon of social work as the numbers of workers increased rapidly throughout the health and welfare services. Although making lists is necessary in order to know what it is that you have, quite what each theory and its practice does, or when it might be used, cannot be answered by reading an inventory.

*A common purpose and the unification of theory*   One way of coping with the overcrowding that was taking place in social work theory was to rationalize. Conceptually, this was very attractive. It would be good to house all social work's explanatory formulae under the same roof. So, was there an underlying theme or unity to social work practice? To help answer such a question, a concept or principle was needed around which rationalization might take place. 'Social functioning' proved to be such a concept.

There was a belief that common to all social work theories and their practice was a shared purpose and concern. Butrym (1976, p.15) feels that the concept of 'social functioning' provided social work with its basic terms of reference in relation to its broad objectives. The individual should be helped to function appropriately and acceptably in society. The race was on to define a 'unified' theory, a unitary approach to practice, one in which the methods of social work could be integrated into a common endeavour.

By the 1970s a whole spate of 'unitary' approaches flooded into social work. From the plethora of theories in the preceding decades, the hope was that common concepts, principles and skills could be extracted which would represent the essence of social work. This 'essence' seemed to fit comfortably into the current fashion of thinking in terms of 'systems'. Systems theory had been having a successful time in biology, ecology and engineering and it seemed just the thing for confused social workers and their knotted practice. Systems theory encouraged practitioners to see their clients and their problems as part of a whole. The behaviour of each component affected, and in its turn was affected by, all other parts of the whole or system. Thus, to treat one problem entailed understanding the functioning of other related parts of the system. So, for example, with the difficult child, the behaviour of his parents, his peers and his school may all have a bearing on his conduct. After a 'systems analysis', the practitioner might well conclude that altering the anti-social outlook of the local peer group is, in fact, the best way to tackle the client's difficult behaviour and not to send him to an educational psychologist.

In spite of the widespread fashion for systems theory throughout the 1970s, the unification of social work theories was premature, incomplete and illusory. It was the product of epistemological myopia. During this same period, radical theories entered the fray. There was also a resurgence of practices that placed high value on the client's view of things: a person-centred, subject-focused, experientially flavoured practice.

Although these trends will be explored later, at this stage it is sufficient to say that the systems-based approaches themselves were making many large assumptions about the state of society, the nature of human beings and the purposes of social work that were not shared by other theories and practices around at that time. It was presumptuous, if not arrogant, to say that social work, theoretically and practically, was being unified. It also profoundly misunderstood the contested ground on which knowledge about people and their society stands. Unifying social work theory is impossible as different theories just look at the world in ways which remain irredeemably incompatible.

This brings us back to familiar territory. Here we meet a number of writers who begin to appreciate that social work's knowledge base is a complex affair. They show the way towards the seventh stage which is where we now find ourselves and the one in which this book is set.

*Classifying social work theories*  In Whittaker's 1974 book, he includes a chapter on the theoretical bases of social treatment. He recognizes that not only does theory inform practice, but also different theories offer contrasting views of human nature and ultimately the purpose of social work itself. Four theories are examined: psychoanalytic, social learning, social systems, and humanistic-existential. Each is analyzed in terms of its major assumptions about human nature and society. 'One thing should be clear,' concludes Whittaker (1974, p.108), 'that the choice of theoretical orientation has a great deal to do with shaping the atmosphere of the therapeutic encounter between client and worker.' This is a useful counter to blithe appeals for integration; but it does not go as far as it might. It is necessary to turn to Leonard, a British author, to help make the final push into the much more agitated, but fog-free waters of social theory.

Leonard (1975) opens his discussion with the following words:

> Not only are rival and conflicting explanations of human and social structure explored in social work education but many of these perspectives are based on different *criteria* of explanation itself . . . It is a major challenge to social work education to provide a means for students to find their way around these different approaches (p.325).

Like most explorers in this area, Leonard finds the concept of a paradigm useful. In a household dictionary you will find that paradigm is defined as a pattern or example. However, in the social sciences it has taken on a more elaborate meaning. In this corner of life it defines a larger concept in which all the assumptions, theories, beliefs, values and methods that make up a particular and preferred view of the world are said to constitute a paradigm.

| PHYSICAL SCIENCES PARADIGM | |
| --- | --- |
| *POSITION A:*<br><br>Social sciences should aspire to status of physical sciences.<br>Importance of measurement and objectivity.<br>Public knowledge is determined by sensory data. | *POSITION B:*<br><br>General similarity of physical and social sciences in objectives and methods.<br>Stress on inexactness of the physical sciences.<br>Importance of probability in both sciences. |
| HUMAN SCIENCES PARADIGM | |
| *POSITION C:*<br><br>Subjective understanding crucial to the social sciences.<br>Questions are value-laden: answers can be relatively value-free. | *POSITION D:*<br><br>Social sciences are socially determined.<br>Ideological influences are central.<br>Importance of studying socio economic context of theories. |

*Figure 3.1*

Source: Leonard 1975.

Leonard recognizes two major types of paradigm: the physical sciences paradigm, and the human sciences paradigm. People approach problems, explain their nature and tackle them in fundamentally different ways depending with which paradigm their sympathies lie. Offering two versions of each, he goes on to explore four possible positions that any social work explanation may take. They are described in Figure 3.1, reproduced from Leonard's original article.

His analysis provides a refreshing clarity of thought about the relationship between theory and practice. Use of some of his examples will be made in a while, but we can refine the framework one more time.

Social theorists, busy worrying about the nature of people and their society, have debated matters along two key dimensions. The first argues whether people are best understood either as objects whose behaviour is essentially determined or as self-respecting subjects who are responsible for their actions: the objective-subjective split. The second argues whether society is most usefully examined as a well-ordered, stable phenomenon or as a fragmented, conflict-ridden entity: the order-conflict debate.

Over the next four chapters we shall consider each of these major dimensions in more detail. They give strong hints on how to think about, understand and classify social work theories, but still fall short of a fully fledged framework. The breakthrough comes in exploring the work of Burrell and Morgan (1979). In Chapter 6 we shall examine their classification of social theory and find that it suits our purposes very well indeed. It will provide a framework in which we shall be able to order and appreciate the full range of social work's current theories. In effect, we find ourselves with a taxonomy of social work theory. This enables us to understand why different theories provide contrasting explanations of the same phenomenon and how their application leads to fundamentally different types of practice.

# 4 The World of Objects and Subjects

So far, two important things about theory have been stated as it is used to negotiate the physical and social world. The first says that a particular phenomenon may receive different explanations according to different theories. The second alerts us to a fascinating and profound notion. It is this. Either, theories seek to discover the real objective nature of things. Or, theories simply reflect the subjectively generated explanations of what things might mean for people who make them. In one scheme we seek to discern the inherent order of the universe. 'Reality' is external to the individual, 'imposing itself on individual consciousness from without' (Burrell and Morgan 1979, p.1). In the other, the human mind imposes its own order on the world as perceived. As it perceives, so the mind conceives. Indeed, as it conceives so it also perceives. It conceives patterns and regularities within and between things, within and between people. The mind does not receive objectivity, it confers it (Cupitt 1985, p.247).

It is to these two opposed orientations that we turn in more detail. As will be seen, the split they provoke reverberates in a particularly noisy fashion through the social and behavioural sciences. The two ways that we think we make sense of people and things have been called the 'objective' and 'subjective'. At this stage it is important to grasp the far-reaching implications of this division in the assumptions made about the nature of knowledge, understanding and social reality. It runs deep throughout the theories of social work and marks off two very different styles of practice.

For example, it is possible to 'understand' and respond to the adolescent delinquent in two different ways. Viewed objectively, a large number of teenage boys who misbehave and commit offences, among other things, come from broken homes, live in poor housing in inner cities and play truant. The social and material environment is said to determine the production of delinquency. The miscreant is merely a victim of his grim surroundings. This 'social problem' might be 'treated' by reducing poverty, improving the quality of housing and preventing children skipping school. Viewed subjectively, individual adolescents may see their behaviour in very personal and idiosyncratic terms. Their actions are designed to interest and satisfy them. Acts that are defined as criminal may simply be seen as 'having a laugh' by the boy. Feelings of excitement outweigh any moral doubts. Or, such bravado enhances the status of the offender in the eyes of his companions. The behaviour, then, makes sense in terms of what the individual and his friends value. Those interested in such behaviour have to enquire of the individual and his peers what it is they believe to be going on. Involvement, whether out of academic curiosity or therapeutic concern, has to start at this subjective level of understanding.

Looking at people and things as either objects or subjects finds us holding contrasting assumptions about the nature of understanding itself. In particular, each dimension says rather different things about what we can know and how we come to know it. Our knowledge of the world, how we acquire that knowledge and what it means is an area of intense debate. Arguments take place on four topics:

1   Human nature − what is it like?
2   The essence of phenomena themselves − what are things like 'in themselves'? This is the business of 'ontology' and is most important when thinking about human beings and their society.
3   The actual grounds of knowledge, that is 'how one might begin to understand the world and communicate this knowledge to other people' (Burrell and Morgan 1979, p.1). These are matters of 'epistemology'.
4   The methods that best 'get at' the knowledge and understanding one is seeking.

Put like this, it all sounds dauntingly abstract. Nevertheless we should stay in the area a while longer. The ideas do actually help us understand why there are different explanations and courses of action proposed in apparently the same situation. Let us rummage a bit deeper into their complexities and then try them out on a social problem or two and see where they take us.

### The objective approach
To those with an objective eye, the social world, as well as the physical, is external to the individual. It is made up of real and concrete structures. 'For the realist, the social world exists independently of an individual's appreciation of it' (Burrell and Morgan 1979, p.4). It exists prior to the individual's personal existence. It has a direct and deterministic bearing on his or her development and circumstances. Thus, we may talk of economic structures creating not just material conditions, but having a pervasive effect on a person's outlook, understanding and awareness of who he or she is.

Seeing the world objectively encourages the observer to look for patterns of behaviour. There is a search for order, regularity and causal links between social phenomena which are external and real. Emile Durkheim, writing around the turn of the century, argues that there are such things as 'social facts'. They are just as real in their effect as any solid physical object. Customs, institutions and beliefs are social facts that influence our individual behaviour. Therefore we can study social facts in the same way that we can examine physical entities.

Investigating the occurrence of suicide, Durkheim sought to demonstrate that it was the result of various social facts combining to produce an individual act of suicide. As different societies contain different arrays of social facts, we should expect suicide rates to vary between cultures. Durkheim pursued his enquiries by analyzing the official statistics on suicide in several European countries. People appeared to be killing themselves more in some countries than others. This suggested to Durkheim that suicide was socially determined. Reflecting on this state of affairs, he believed that the amount of social integration enjoyed by a society determined its number of 'voluntary deaths'. The greater the level of social integration, measured by the number and closeness of relationships with other people, the less alone is each individual who is therefore not so disposed to end it all. Durkheim found that suicide was more prevalent in Protestant countries than Catholic, in urban societies than rural, and amongst the unmarried rather than the married. On the basis of the reasoning employed, social integration is lower in Protestant, urban and single personal groupings. So, even though killing oneself appears to be an intensely personal act, its causes are to be found in the nature of social groups and the forces which they generate in the realms of friendship, community and intimacy. Our behaviour is the product of the type of society in which we live. A vast amount of sociological enquiry sets about the social world in this manner. Thus, unemployment is seen to cause city riots, violence on television may produce muggings in the streets and hard pornography may create the sexual perverts that roam the night.

Human nature for the objectivist is determined by the individual's genetic inheritance and biological predisposition ('nature'). It is also determined by the individual's experiences both as he or she develops and as they currently pertain ('nurture'). The quality of parenting, the material conditions enjoyed, the standard of education, the character of the language environment all have a direct bearing on the way people turn out, socially and psychologically. People in this argument are either born or made or both. We are the products of our environment for good or ill.

Hollis (1977) dubs this model of human nature 'Plastic Man'. Here, naturalism and determinism go happily together. Underlying human behaviour are universal laws. We are essentially passive creatures. We are natural and determined phenomenon just as much as the rocks, plants and animals around us. Our behaviour is therefore predictable in given situations. Plastic Man is programmed and can be conditioned. Behaviour can be manipulated and changed by altering the environment. Improving people's housing, raising their wealth, providing nursery schools or punishing misdemeanours can alter what they do and so shift the character of their social conduct.

## The subjective approach

For the subjectivist, the 'sense and order' to be found in natural objects and people's behaviour is created in people's minds. They devise patterns and relationships of more or less usefulness to help them steady their perceptions. It helps them find their bearings in what would otherwise be an unpredictable place. Meaning is imposed by men and women on things and people. Knowledge is gained through personal experience. There are no inherent natural regularities in people's behaviour or social affairs. How the world is or appears can only be understood from the point of view of the people directly involved in whatever activity is being considered. We 'can only "understand" by occupying the frame of reference of the participant in action' (Burrell and Morgan 1979, p.5). In this way, anthropologists are disposed to join tribes and live on South Sea islands. Sociologists leave their ivory towers and become honorary members of street corner gangs, better to understand the delinquent and his fellows. We construct our own social reality. Meaning arises as we mix and relate to other people. There are no social facts, only meanings which are generated in the interactions between people.

So, what does the subjectivist make of suicide? Atkinson (1971 and 1978) answers the question along the following lines. Social events take on their meaning according to what those involved make of them. Suicide is the description of some deaths (but not others) as defined by particular actors in the situation. For a death to be labelled as suicide depends on the perceptions and definitions made by doctors, coroners, policemen and the deceased's family. Rather than assume that there is an objective act of suicide, Atkinson prefers to ask 'How do deaths get categorised as suicide?' What are the characteristics of the situation which encourage or discourage people to see someone's death as an act of suicide? Once we start thinking in the spirit prompted by these sort of questions, it soon becomes apparent that calling a death suicide is a tricky decision. Some individuals will deliberately disguise their suicide to look like an accident. How many car deaths on lonely roads were successful bids to finish with life? Families, too, prefer a verdict of accidental death, feeling that suicide carries the mark of a stigma. Whereas suicide may be a sinful act on the part of a Catholic, it does not receive the same censure by a Protestant community. Classifying a death as suicide in Dublin or Rome may be more than just an official statistic, it may suggest that the unhappy fellow is doomed to an eternity of hellfire and damnation. It seems only prudent to see his demise as a case of accident or misadventure.

Official records, then, are not necessarily wrong. They are simply a report of how a particular society chooses to look at the deaths of some of its members.

Atkinson's own research took him into the offices of coroners and the courts where inquests were being held. In both these settings there were 'commonsense' theories of suicide being used. If the deceased possessed certain characteristics his or her death was more likely to be seen as suicide. The following indicated that suicide was the more likely verdict: drug overdose (but not a road accident), previous threats of suicide, and history of mental disturbance. One coroner said to Atkinson, 'there's a classic pattern for you — broken home, escape to the services, nervous breakdown, unsettled at work, no family ties — what could be clearer'. None of this is to deny that some people do deliberately take their own lives. What is at issue is which people, why and says who. For the subjectivist, such events and what they mean, to actors and observers alike, can only be understood at the level of individual subjectivities. That is where one's enquiries must turn if one is to understand what is going on.

With the subjective approach, human nature enjoys free will. Hollis (1977) calls this self-determining individual 'Autonomous Man'. Such a person interprets, reflects, plans, decides, acts intentionally and is responsible for his choices.

> Whereas Plastic Man, being formed by adaptive response to the interplay of nature and nurture, is only spuriously individual, his rival is to be self-caused. Where Plastic Man is an object in nature, his rival is the 'I' of the I and Me. Where Plastic Man has his causes, Autonomous Man has his reasons (ibid., p.12).

In order to understand the other person, we must learn of his reasons; and to change things for that person, we must plan *with* him and not *for* him. Other people's actions are determined by them. They are not subject to causal laws. This has deep implications for the way the social worker approaches, understands and works with her clients. They should be approached as independent operators, with their own views, feelings and ideas about what is going on and what might be done. People define their own situations. They make their own interpretation of events. These must not be ignored if the social worker is to have an appropriate and worthwhile part to play.

## The case of juvenile delinquency and social work practice

Taking note of what has been said so far, the social worker can see a situation in one of two ways in the light of which she can act in one of two ways. The division between people seen as either objects or subjects colours the way she identifies problems, explains what is going on and chooses methods of intervention.

Let us take adolescents who misbehave as an example. Teenage criminals have concerned and irritated many societies. A vast range of explanations and consequent responses have arisen. Using the ideas of this chapter, we can contrast two major views of deviance. One is set within the causal tradition of the scientist. The other takes a subjectivist approach. As will be seen, each view leads to a very different type of practice.

Many psychological theories view the young criminal as an object of scientific study. His behaviour is self-evidently taken as abnormal. In some ways he is 'sick' and needs to be treated and cured. Although historically there are theories that seek to show that criminality is genetically transmitted, the abnormal behaviour is now more likely to be seen as the result of faulty learning. Poor developmental experiences produce 'character disorders' and 'maladjusted personalities'. There are a large number of theories and practices which derive from them, but those associated with John Bowlby can be taken as typical. They have certainly been influential.

He believes the nurturing relationship between mother and child to be naturally necessary. Good mental health in adult life is the result of the infant and child experiencing 'a warm, intimate and continuous relationship with his mother' (Haralambos 1985, p.372). Any disruption of this relationship disturbs that child's proper emotional development; he suffers maternal deprivation. These poor childhood experiences scar the adolescent's personality. He is unable to give and receive love. His behaviour is inclined to be impulsive, antisocial and pays little heed to the consequences. Bowlby believes that children who did not enjoy sufficient motherly love and emotional security, perhaps because they were brought up in a large residential home or were raised in turbulent, unstable and emotionally precarious households, were likely candidates for a life of crime and wrongdoing.

This explanation of delinquency inspired the apocryphal tales of young offenders telling magistrates that they were not responsible for their criminal deeds; they were the products of broken homes. For those dealing with children in trouble, this theoretical understanding of the problem involved taking a detailed account of the offender's personal history. If the current behaviour is the result of 'acting out' disturbed emotional experiences, treatment plans require a thorough knowledge of the disturbances that upset their upbringing. Since the cause of the problem is deep-rooted, there are no quick and easy solutions. Therapy requires slow, steady and reassuring responses to compensate for the inconsistent love and care received in the past. The environment needs to offer emotional security. Relationships between the social worker and the delinquent should promote trust and acceptance. This allows the client to work through, strengthen and gain insight into his emotional weaknesses.

Many residential regimes approach the needs of young people in similar style. They provide warm, caring, nurturing settings. Food, attention and acceptance are provided in comfortable surroundings. Under these conditions, the emotionally deprived adolescent can retrace his childhood experiences in a safe, consistent environment. He can recover emotional coherence and integrity. His psychological development can be repaired. If this therapeutic experience is successful, he will be able to rejoin the world as a self-controlled, content, trusting and responsive human being.

In contrast, there are those who think that the best way to understand the young criminal is to see how things look from his point of view. Taking the subjective line, behaviour that is regarded as deviant in itself is not indicative of any psychological abnormality. It is a chosen course of action which just happens to upset other members of society. Although there are many social theories, like psychological ones, which see the deviant as the passive product of forces beyond his control, a reaction has grown to this style of explanation. It recognizes that the individual is capable of choice. He has responsibility for his actions. His behaviour is neither passive, nor simply determined. In his review of David Matza's sociology of delinquency, Haralambos (1985, pp.422−5) describes the argument that, like many teenagers, the delinquent is in search of excitement, that aggression is a demonstration of masculinity. Many young people simply 'drift' into delinquency. They are not committed to it or bound to behave badly.

However, those sociologists known as 'interactionists' go on to look at the relationship between those who are seen as deviant and those who describe them as deviant. There is nothing inherently criminal about a delinquent adolescent. Rather, the 'nature' of the deviant is defined in the interactions which take place, say between the police, the school, the media and the boys themselves. Each participant holds a view about what is going on, what is wrong and what should be done. What the young offender's behaviour 'means' is the result of what other people believe is really happening. It is not a manifestation of his inherent criminal nature. This is why interactionists say that deviancy is socially manufactured.

Perhaps the most famous quote to emerge out of this school of thought comes from Howard S. Becker (1963). It sums up the essential ingredients of the interactionist's analysis:

> *Social groups create deviance by making the rules whose infraction constitutes deviance,* and by applying those rules to particular people and labelling them as outsiders. From this point of view, deviance is not a quality of the act the person commits, but rather a consequence of the application by others of the rules and sanctions to an 'offender'. The deviant is the one to whom the label has successfully been applied; deviant behaviour is behaviour that people so label (ibid.).

Becker reminds us that adolescents are inclined to mess about, brawl and fight. In working class areas, this may indicate delinquent tendencies. However, the same behaviour by the children of the rich, say in the neighbourhood of a public school, is defined as youthful high spirits and jolly japes. What a behaviour 'means' depends upon the context in which it occurs. Furthermore, those who are carrying out the behaviour, such as the fighting in our case, will also have views about what is taking place. The working class boys see themselves as defending their territory. They are doing only what they consider necessary and right. However, teachers, social workers and police may well see it differently. Once the label of deviant has been attached to the individual, he is treated according to the characteristics 'known' to be associated with deviance. To some extent, the individual is then trapped within the confines of the label. Whatever behaviour he offers, it is likely to be seen as further evidence of his wayward tendencies and so further confirms the true nature of his 'character'.

Understanding adolescent misbehaviour as a product of social inter-action, and not as a fixed quality of the individual, has influenced the practice of many social workers. If the origins of deviance lie within the interactions between the alleged deviant and the agents of social control, it follows that this relationship needs to be changed. For example, bringing young offenders into the criminal justice system should be avoided whenever possible. It only compounds the problem. Alternatives to immediate prosecution, court and custody should be worked out. The miscreants themselves are encouraged to consider not so much the rightness or wrongness of their actions, but what the consequences appear to be.

In such approaches, it is not intended to change the adolescent himself. There is nothing wrong with his functioning. What is changed are the social arrangements and responses that surround his behaviour. This alters the meaning of what he does. As has been seen, the argument is that what a behaviour 'means' is entirely relative to the situation in which it occurs.

## Conclusion

The two theoretical approaches give rise to different explanations and lead to different practices. Followers of Bowlby do a repair and recovery job. Those impressed with the arguments of the interactionists change the perspective and so change the definition of what is seen to be normal and abnormal. A flimsy car may fall to pieces on a rough road. It may need extensive strengthening, tougher wheels and more robust shock absorbers if it is to survive. The alternative answer lies in making the road smoother and life altogether less bumpy. The practitioner as therapist and the practitioner as social planner have a long and established tradition in social work. However, their practices stem from contrasting outlooks on the nature and origin of social behaviour.

# 5 Order and Conflict in Society

Observers of society are disposed to reflect on it in one of two ways. There are those who wonder at the orderliness, stability and persistence of human affairs; and there are others who see conflict, discord and change as the very stuff of social living. Again, our main purpose is to recognize that different theories lead to different practices. However, this time our attention will be focused on the degree of equilibrium said to be exhibited by a social system.

The two assumptions about the nature of society have been contrasted in what has been called the 'order-conflict' debate. In the world of practice, each assumption sponsors methods designed either to restore equilibrium or to promote fundamental change. Burrell and Morgan (1979, pp.10–19) review the debate. They reformulate the contrast in terms of (i) a sociology of regulation and (ii) a sociology of radical change. Just as there are those who see their glass as half empty and those who see it as half full, so, in looking at the world of people, there are those who prefer to recognize the settled rhythms of everyday life and those who are ever alert to the self-interest, tension and injustices that burden the human condition. Whether the aim is to keep the social wheels turning smoothly or to rejig the whole works, we need to understand the contrast in the assumptions which underlie these two views on the nature of society. 'They reflect fundamentally different frames of reference. They present themselves, therefore, as alternative models for the analysis of social processes' (Burrell and Morgan 1979, p.18).

### Regulation and order in social life

The remarkable thing about human society is the ability of thousands and millions of people to live and work together in some well-ordered, integrated fashion. Whether in families or giant organizations, a feeling of co-operation and common purpose exists. Individuals and groups contribute to the overall functioning of society. Their activities mesh and cohere so that we can talk of society, organization and social institutions − complex social arrangements that persist over time.

There are families to rear the young and schools to train them. Children turn up at the classroom each morning with a teacher waiting, ready to give them instruction. Skills and values, ideas and practices are transmitted to each generation thereby sustaining the momentum of a well-functioning society. There are places to work and systems of transport. Houses are built and financial organizations evolve to help rent or buy them. While one person treats the sick, another removes the rubbish thrown out by our consumer society. Social order, consensus and equilibrium are impressive achievements and, sociologically speaking, require explanation.

The term 'sociology of regulation' refers to the work of theorists who explain society in terms that emphasize its 'underlying unity and cohesiveness' and why it 'tends to hold together rather than fall apart' (Burrell and Morgan 1979, p.17). Thinking about society along these lines has encouraged analogies with the natural and mechanical world. So, society is said to function like a body, organically. *Structures* refer to the complex whole, the way in which society is held together. *Function* considers what individual parts or 'organs' do in relation to each other. 'So', write Cashmore and Mullen (1983) reviewing this approach:

> Societies are thought to be complexes of parts, or institutions like the economy, religion, or politics, working together and yielding a healthy functioning whole . . . Spencer detailed three vital functions important to the survival of any society: regulation -- they have to be governed; distribution -- goods have to be produced and circulated; sustenance -- populations have to be reproduced in orderly sequence (p.135).

Governments, economies and families help fulfil these functions. The function of any recurrent activity, such as the punishment of a crime, a funeral ceremony or a wedding, is the part it plays in the social life as a whole. It therefore contributes to the maintenance of social order and stability. Thus, the functionalist examines a part of society, such as the family, in terms of its contribution to the support of the social system. For example, families help socialize new members into the expected, preferred, accepted and proper ways of behaving in society. Perhaps the clearest, earliest and most articulate expression of this style of social analysis was given by Emile Durkheim (1855-1917) in what came to be known as 'structural functionalism'.

Such a view of society presumes that all the parts and what they do work for the common good. Even though we all do different jobs, like the organs of the body, we seek to keep the whole social enterprise going for our own sakes as well as for the sake of the whole. Other people need us, but we need other people. There is so much specialization or division of labour in the modern world that society is kept together because everyone is dependent on everyone else. Our roles intertwine and wrap around one another in such density that a kind of social solidarity results. Built into this account of society is a vast complex of mutual expectations. Norms and values underpin our social performances. We learn what is expected of us in the family, at school, in the workplace and through the media.

If we do not behave in the ways expected of, say, a parent or school-child, we are seen as poor functioners, neglectful of our social duties. In order to ensure the overall wellbeing of the social whole, the system, through its laws and welfare agents, seeks to return the individual to a proper state of social functioning, namely a caring parent or non-truanting schoolchild. Pressures, both formal and informal, are brought to bear. Policemen, social workers and officials of all kinds become interested in those who stray from the established standards of good conduct, self-care and financial independence. What a society values must be upheld and affirmed. If the methods of control and correction fail, the individual who 'malfunctions' will be isolated from the social body. He will lie outside normal society. Inveterate nonconformists languish in prison, psychiatric hospitals and fringe communities, they doss under city bridges and they plot as rebels on the political margins where they threaten the values and assumptions built into everyday 'normal' life.

## Conflict and social change

The harmony extolled in the well-ordered society is not recognized in the conflict model. Or if it is, it flourishes as an illusion conjured up by the powerful to beguile the weak into accepting a profoundly unequal order in which the strong are the prime beneficiaries. The radical theorist attempts to see through the illusion.

In this view of society, strife is a major characteristic of social life. People compete for limited resources. Interests clash. Different groups hold different ideas about what is best or fair or appropriate. Whereas differences, divisions and inequalities are said to hold society together in the functionalist model, here they threaten to pull it apart. Alignments and intentions change as individuals regroup to further their own concerns. Workers go on strike for more pay while those who own capital try to keep things the way they are. Laws may favour some sections of society more than others: in the radical analysis there is indeed one law for the rich and another for the poor. Social values are not shared as the sociology of regulation believes. Values are imposed. Hence the interest in power and how some groups exercise control, often implicitly, over others. In fact the powerful set the ideological climate in which laws are made, values promulgated and ideas established, a climate that blows fair for the classes that rule but which chills the prospects of the weak.

It is rarely possible for the strong completely to hoodwink the weak. It is these feelings of unfairness and inequality that fuel conflict. The result of these political and economic manoeuvrings is the phenomenon of social change. Societies are possessed of a restless quality in which people and their ideas are never still. Conflict and change are endemic. Attempts to explain the shifting fortunes of various social groups lead to a very different crop of theories to those that tackle the problem of order.

The basic concern of the 'sociology of radical change' is to explain fundamental social movements, 'deep-seated structural conflict, modes of domination and structural contradiction which its theorists see as characterising modern society' (Burrell and Morgan 1979, p.17). In order to appreciate how events develop, the theorist needs to adopt a historical perspective. Cashmore and Mullen (1983) illustrate this point with the following example:

> The downfall of feudal society came through opposition between a new, rising group of mercantile urban dwellers and the traditional group of landed artistocrats. There was a basic conflict in the interests of the two groups. As the mercantilists gained more resources, they were able to seize power from the feudal lords and clear away obstacles to their own enterprises. For example, old laws relating to land which were tailored to suit feudalists' interests were changed to meet the new mercantilists' need to create more wealth (p.148).

In modern times, the fundamental conflict of interest lies between those who own capital and the means of production on the one hand and the working classes who have no choice but to work for them on the other. This not only sets up economic conflict, but also leads to ideological and psychological tensions in the minds of those involved. That is, the forces and relationship of production produce an economic structure which shapes the political, legal and educational climate in which people live and grow. Every aspect of life is affected by the profound inequalities to be found in the economic system. There is tension in the family, there is hostility to school, aggression in the workplace.

Those who do the work in modern factories with fast-moving production lines and extensive divisions of labour have no control over what they make or how they make it. In the work of Marx this is said to have a profound effect on the minds of men and women. If workers are detached from the objects that they make, they become alienated from the products of their own labour. Work should be creative, an expression of the worker's own being. If work becomes fragmented, it also becomes meaningless and without satisfaction. The worker's outlook becomes limited, constrained, one-dimensional. The divided opportunities of the economic world have their counterpart in the consciousness of people and the divisions that arise between them:

> The mode of production in material life determines the general character of the social, political and spiritual processes of life. It is not the consciousness of men that determines their existence, but, on the contrary, their social existence determines their consciousness (Marx 1859 in 1977, p.21).

In order to explain, radical theorists look back, but their eye is also firmly fixed on the future. They want change, radical change. They have a powerful vision of the future in which the full potential of human beings is realized in a new order of economic production and hence social arrangements whether at work, play or in the family. Thus, the current order is not accepted. Power in the community can be redistributed. Officials, including social workers, do not necessarily know best: theirs need not be the only definition of what is right, good and proper.

People can fight for change at all economic, political and social levels. Whenever established, dominant interests masquerade as equitable, fair and free; there is the prospect of exposure, challenge, conflict and ultimately change. Radical analyses reveal who is benefiting from established arrangements. They trace how domination is sustained and suggest what must be done to bring about shifts in power, interests and resources. Before the deprived or ill-served can be helped, the effective practitioner needs to establish who holds the power, whose interests are being furthered and what devices are used to keep things the way they are. Only when the various interests have been mapped, and the power relationship laid bare, can the aggrieved determine possible courses of action.

## Example: order, conflict and the child at school

Order and conflict, equilibrium and change provide alternative frames of understanding people and the way they live in society. For example, family life or the workings of the criminal justice system receive markedly different explanations by functionalists and Marxists. However, the schoolchild and the educational system will be used to highlight the contrasts in the two accounts of society.

Between the ages of five and sixteen children have to attend school. For up to seven hours a day, five days a week, they are in the classroom or on the playing field. Society spends a great deal of time and money on educating its children. Without a doubt, the educational experience is a major event in the lives of children, their parents and the community. The quality of this experience is of great interest to many people. Teachers, child welfare agents, parents, potential employers and the children themselves express views and make judgements on what has taken place. So, although school may simply be just a way of passing the time between nine and four o'clock each day, at least as far as some children and their parents are concerned, others do not view it so casually. Considerable attention is paid to the way the child handles his schooldays. Does he actually go to school? How does he behave when he is there? How well does he perform, academically and socially? Is he a good member of the school community?

The fact that a child's performance at school is taken as an indication of what the rest of his character is like is interestingly demonstrated by the work of Ball (1981). She investigated the making of care orders in a juvenile court. Nineteen boys and one girl, with ages ranging between twelve and sixteen, were all charged at various times over an eighteen-month period with offences involving theft of property. All were placed in the care of the local authority.

As well as the usual social enquiry report, the court was also provided with a report prepared by his or her school. Ball:

> Discovered that the magistrates' decision to impose care orders appeared to be influenced more by the contents of the school report and by reference to educational factors in the social enquiry report than by other social work factors (ibid., p.480).

The factors assessed as primarily influencing the making of a care order included such things as 'disruptive behaviour in school', 'suspended from school' and 'persistent truanting'. 'The most common blanket formula by which chairmen met their obligations under rule ten was to the effect that "the report from your school is not very good — have you anything to say about that".' Thus, it appears that the way a child handles his schooling allows a broader judgement to be made about his fitness to tackle the wider business of living in society in a responsible, useful and acceptable manner.

Theories set within the sociology of regulation and the sociology of radical change approach education and its role in society from opposite directions. They promote contrasting understandings of the school, the child and society. Skipping class or misbehaving in maths seen one way is a problem *for* the school, seen another it becomes a problem *of* the school. Depending inside which theoretical framework the observer is sited, ideas about what should be done about it are inclined not only to vary, but to clash.

We shall take the position of the 'functionalist' as one concerned with the part education plays in the maintenance of society and social order. Marxists take us firmly into the camp of radical change where we shall be much keener to spot what education does *to* the child rather than *for* him.

### Social order: socializing and assessing children

Education performs two basic functions for society. Firstly, it transmits ideas about which behaviours are wanted and valued, which behaviours are acceptable and rewarded. This produces people who think in similar ways about work, needs, conduct and performance. Out of this comes a sense of belonging to a like-minded group, a society of common interests and understandings. This results in social unity. The second basic function that education performs for society is that the education system prepares people for the economic system. It grades people's skills and abilities, providing a fit between the stratification of work and the hierarchy of talent. This is efficient, appropriate and necessary if society is to make the best use of the abilities of the new generation: horses for courses.

For example, Durkheim said that:

> It is by respecting the school rules that the child learns to respect rules in general, that he develops the habit of self-control and restraint simply because he should control and restrain himself. It is a first initiation into the austerity of duty. Serious life has now begun.

Schools complement the functions of the family by 'socializing' the child, instructing him or her in the accepted ways and habits of their society. Children are prepared for their adult roles. What goes on in the classroom is in fact a microcosm of what is to happen in the wider world of work, rewards and sociable living. This is why what happens at schools is of vital concern to society as a whole if it is to function smoothly. Herbert (1978, p.241) reports the work of Robins on this theme. He shows, for example, that a child's attendance record at school is a very good predictor of his adult adjustment.

If the educational system is about preparing minds and bodies to find a place in society, children who fail to respond appropriately are a problem. They will not be contributing to the functioning of the community. Indeed, they may unsettle its smooth working and loosen the solidarity that is so important if society is to maintain its social order.

Some children fight the values and assumptions that underlie the educational enterprise. They do not seek academic achievements. There is no respect for authority. School is felt to be irrelevant. Some may fail to learn how to blend into the classroom hierarchy. They do not even attempt the practical, intellectual and social skills that are required if the school's *raison d'être* is to be upheld. Rutter (1975, p.268) describes such children as suffering 'learning disorders'. In order to work, the life of the classroom depends on the teacher and pupil acquiring and accepting a number of ground rules. These include attendance, attention, acceptance of authority and a willingness to learn what is taught. If a child has problems in these areas they belong to him. For whatever reasons, he is at fault. If he has a problem, he is the problem.

If the child fails to turn up at school, an educational welfare officer is called in to investigate. If the child cannot function along the required lines, he or she is regarded as difficult. In extreme cases the child is referred to a child psychiatrist who may diagnose him to be 'maladjusted'. The Underwood Report on maladjusted children was quite clear about the need to identify and treat such children. 'Pupils who show evidence of emotional instability or psychological disturbance and require special educational treatment in order to effect their personal, social or education readjustment' are defined as maladjusted (in Robinson 1978, p.120).

Clearly, the proper socialization of the child is the goal of many of those who work in schools, child welfare agencies and health departments. Children who do not respond to the socialization process have to be treated if they are to fit successfully into society. To this end, psychologists work out programmes of 'desensitization' to help a school phobic return to the classroom. 'There is a greater appreciation nowadays,' notes Herbert (1978, p.242), 'that some forms of school refusal constitute a very real emotional or conduct disorder.' More conventionally, truants are told that if they carry on missing school and end up with no qualifications they will never get a job; no one will look at them.

Overall, it appears that performance at school is taken as a major indicator of a child's fitness to be in society, to be seen as socially competent and responsible. As well as the educational welfare officer, the psychiatrist and the psychologist, the problem schoolchild may also see the arrival of the social worker. She is the person designated as responsible for overseeing the proper development and general well-being of children in our society. Not doing well at school is a definite sign that a child is not functioning properly. This observation crops up in court reports, assessment papers and review documents. Robinson (1978) has written a whole book all about the child, the social worker and the school. She is quite clear about the issues. They are captured in one of the book's major sections entitled 'Social functioning and social breakdown'. Like families, schools, she believes, are agents of socialization:

> This concept of socialisation is of equal use to teachers and social workers and may provide one of the bridges towards the development of mutual understanding. Socialisation is the development of the person as a social being and participant in society. It is a process in which different social institutions have their part to play . . . Socialisation agents, when acting also as agents of social control, have responsibilities in relation to maintaining the prevailing moral norms as decreed at macro level (ibid., pp.13–14).

The aims of school teachers and social workers are, therefore, to promote the social functioning of individuals, to help them live up to the expectations of society (ibid., p.39). Whenever the social worker moves in, her aim is to recover the child's ability to function in the educational system. If the child or his family fail to respond or refuse to accept the values that underpin the educational experience, then the social worker shifts into a tougher gear, that of agent of social control. The law requires children to go to school. If 'he is of compulsory school age and is not receiving efficient full-time education suitable to his age, ability and aptitude' the social worker can institute care proceedings which may result in the child being removed from his family and placed in a community home with education.

Throughout the functionalist's analysis, the attention is directed at the 'difficult' child. It is he who is expected to change his ways. It is his inability to cope with school which is a clear indication that he is not likely to fit comfortably into society. His attitude is wrong. Tyerman, for example, believes that truancy is a warning that a child may be having emotional problems. 'At least half the children who play truant,' he argues, 'are maladjusted and one in two commit offences' (in Robinson 1978, pp.144–5). Until he returns to normal functioning, he is denied the full rewards and privileges that conformity brings. Assessments such as 'maladjusted', 'experiencing learning difficulties' and 'problem child' appeal to psychology for a frame of explanation. The aim is to cure a pathological condition.

Let us reverse the perspective. Instead of accepting that there is harmony and social order between the child, the school and society, let us now consider social conflict and how the educational system coerces and manipulates the child to suit the interests of the established and powerful. Tension and conflict simmer in this social brew with the threat that the mixture may boil over at any time.

## Social conflict: education and social control

In preparing children, schools are influenced by the needs of the economic system. In turn, the economic system serves the interests of those who hold the power. Developments in education match developments in industry, commerce and the production of capital. Under the subheading of 'the nature of education destined for the working class', Corrigan (1979, pp.33–4) identifies a number of strands in the 'educational' prescriptions written to treat the threat of insurrection amongst the lower orders:

1 The provision of bourgeois facts and theories to counter both 'revolutionary' facts and those facts that were derived from the material conditions of working-class existence at the time.
2 The provision of a bourgeois moral and religious code which, once it had been taught to the working class, would shape their behaviour.
3 The creation of a disciplined, punctual workforce.
4 The creation of a hierarchy of civilization based upon education and refinement which the working class would respect and of which they would find themselves at the very bottom.

Sharp and Green (1975, p.vii) explore this ground as they see how wider structural 'forces' penetrate all levels of education. In order to demonstrate the relationship between social power and education, they went into the primary school. What goes on between the teacher and her pupil is not a free professional act, as the phenomenologists would have us believe. Rather, it is an encounter saturated with the dominant values and assumptions that flow throughout the whole of social life. 'For us', write Sharp and Green:

> The social world is structured not merely by language and meaning but by the mode and forces of material production and the system of domination which is related in some way to material reality and its control (ibid.).

Social control is maintained through the initiation of pupils, teachers and parents into appropriate attitudes and behaviours.

The sociologist in the classroom must appreciate that, from the texts that are used to the power hierarchy of the school, the outside is fully present in all that is going on:

> We shall see how the teachers' processing of the pupil is related to the structure of material and social constraints on the one hand and to the available 'knowledge' which dictates how the situation should be defined and how the teacher should act within it, on the other hand (ibid., p.33).

Those with the power, be they government ministers, directors of education, headteachers in their school or teachers in their classroom, can define how things are and have to be for others. Children who, for whatever reasons, lie outside this proffered version of educational normality represent a problem with which the system has to deal:

> Thus, whilst the teachers display a moral concern that every child matters, in practice there is a subtle process of sponsorship developing where opportunity is being offered to some and closed off to others. Social stratification is emerging (ibid., p.218).

In their conclusion, Sharp and Green believe that, within the child-centred progressive education, all the child's attributes are used to construct his success or failure:

> Not merely intellectual but social, emotional, aesthetic and even physical criteria are often employed in the processing of pupils in educational institutions, the social control possibilities thus being enhanced. Moreover the development of a quasi therapeutic orientation to the educational task which we have suggested characterises much of 'progressive child centred' thought, impugns those who fail in ways which are non-threatening to established interests, thus 'cooling people out' and moving more and more people into soft control areas (ibid., p.225).

Corrigan (1979) picks up another group of schoolchildren, this time all working class boys living in Sunderland, aged between fourteen and fifteen: the 'Smash Street Kids'. He wonders why some of them play truant, why most of them 'muck about' in class. He shows that the boys do not believe in the myth of equal opportunity. They experience school as 'repression and organise themselves against its power'. They know that school is compulsory. Education is felt to be an imposition by those with power. For many of the boys, the teachers were 'big heads'; people charged by the educational system to 'rule' over their behaviour and intentions. The idea of school was not perceived as much to do with academic teaching and learning, but the installation of self-regulatory behaviour, 'good' and 'civilized' conduct. Backing this attempt was a system of authority and power designed to control their conduct. All of this — being decent and civilized in a middle-class sort of way, obeying rules, respecting authority, accepting educational meritocracy — puts a strain on pupils and teachers alike. According to Corrigan, a major preoccupation of teachers is pupil surveillance:

> Rule-enforcement and rule-breaking become a totally creative process linked to the different sorts of power involved in the situation. The power and imagination of the controlled are pitted against the power and imagination of the controlling (ibid., p.69).

An education system which is designed to change and civilize the behaviour of working class boys means that 'the conflict that ensues is written into every school' (ibid., p.70).

The nature and assumptions of the system provoke or define the behaviour of many children. The mischievous, the unresponsive and the outright disobedient are indeed a problem for the school. 'Experts' who regard such behaviour as abnormal and the product of individual pupil pathology only feed into the prevailing definitions of what is proper, expected and acceptable. Corrigan prefers to understand working class teenage boys waging a kind of guerilla warfare in the school, acts of adolescent resistance against a coercive power that wants them to behave in ways which suit it. The disaffection of adolescent boys is the result of the educational system separating the values it promulgates from the day-to-day experiences of working class youth.

Corrigan feels bound to offer advice. The political right would like tougher discipline back in our schools. Corrigan, however, reminds his more assiduous readers that this, of course, simply provokes more of the thing that it purports to cure. He is equally critical of the 'ultra-left'. They do not accept that it is possible to tinker with the educational system in isolation. If the educational system is simply a method of holding down the potential dissidence of the working classes through coercion and ideological indoctrination, the only real answer for the 'ultra-left' is to go for total revolution, the complete overthrow of society. This would necessarily involve schools and what they currently stand for. For most practitioners, whether teachers or social workers, this course of action is tricky. It is certainly drastic. It feels distant and seems to offer no answers about what to do about Class 3D tomorrow. Corrigan turns to politically less extreme remedies. He advises three groups of people what to do.

Teachers should understand that youth today is confused about what is expected of it. Therefore teachers should understand the changing nature of the world of work and the demands it places on children. Educators 'should listen to the rest of the working class about education' (ibid., p.153). Schools should actively include parents, the local community and political parties in their thoughts and plans about the problems of education and the nature of education in today's capitalist society. Schoolchildren, too, should see some purpose in education, 'see some point in the power that literacy and knowledge give them. This they cannot be *forced* into; they have to be won to the importance of it' (ibid., p.153). Instead of being told what to do and feeling pushed around, they should be invited into the challenge of working out ways to cope, succeed and determine the relevance of what goes on in the school. We should also all stop looking for scapegoats. We should try to understand how pupils, teachers and school are enmeshed in the prevailing system of education. We have to understand the way things are in order to raise our consciousnesses of what is going on before we can change it. Elsewhere, Corrigan, along with Leonard, enlarges on these prescriptions. They examine the work of Pauline, a fictitious social worker dealing with Derek, a thirteen-year-old boy who has been missing school. They make the following comments:

> She relates to school in a simplistic way by seeing it is an oppressive state apparatus; in this particular case, an institution which seems dedicated to getting at Derek, to try to restrict his activities; she even treats the teachers as conscious agents in this restriction and oppression . . . Social workers often fail . . . to appreciate the real work constraints of teachers . . . An analysis of education may lead us to see it as an ideological state apparatus, but also one with progressive contradictions . . . Her primarily negative attitude gets nowhere: it leaves Derek in trouble; it leaves the school untouched; it creates ill-feeling between Pauline and the teachers. Sooner or later, she must progress beyond that negativity and contribute to a structured politics of education and inter-professional activity. Unless the Left in social work starts this work soon, it will be not only preventing the possibility of some real advances for its consumers, but will be missing natural allies, the teachers, in the struggles to come (Corrigan and Leonard 1978, pp.43–4).

It is evident that this radical analysis treads a more rugged path to that taken by those who accept the *status quo*. Whether or not their route is feasible, it is the case that their explanation of the problem schoolchild prompts an entirely different outlook on the theory and practice of social work with difficult children.

The problem, the analysis and the action arising out of the analysis demand an appreciation of social structures and not the identification of wayward personalities. In this frame, the questions to ask are: Who holds the power? How do they exercise it? What is its effect? Can it be challenged? Can it be redistributed? If power can be shifted around, how might the new structures look?

## Conclusion

The two sociologies — one of regulation and the other of conflict — stand us on different ground in order to view people and their circumstances. A useful guide to which side of this broad, but fundamental sociological divide the social worker is likely to lie is given in answer to the following sorts of question. When we have a problem, how do we describe it? What sort of problem is it? Who is it a problem for? What do they want doing about it? Who is to be involved in resolving the problem?

It will be apparent from the type of answers given what assumptions lie behind the way the problem is identified and the methods chosen to tackle it. It is also time to remind ourselves of the central theme of this book: where we site ourselves determines our point of view and our point of view influences our course of action. Perception, conception and action are intimately linked, bound as they are inside their own theoretical order. What we do with our social work clients is not a matter of self-evident commonsense. It is a matter of theoretical choice, whether we care to recognize it or not. Hence the insistence on geography lessons in epistemology.

# 6 A Taxonomy of Social Work Theories

**Two dimensions, four paradigms**

It has been seen that sociological debates easily become trapped along one or other of two conceptual dimensions. Protagonists either argue the merits and demerits of society based on notions of order and conflict; or they split over whether people and their society should be understood 'subjectively' or 'objectively'. The trick worked by Burrell and Morgan (1979) was to combine these two dimensions. They squared them and generated four paradigms, producing a strong grid with powerful analytical properties. The result is described in Figure 6.1. The framework's four distinct paradigms help analyze social theory.

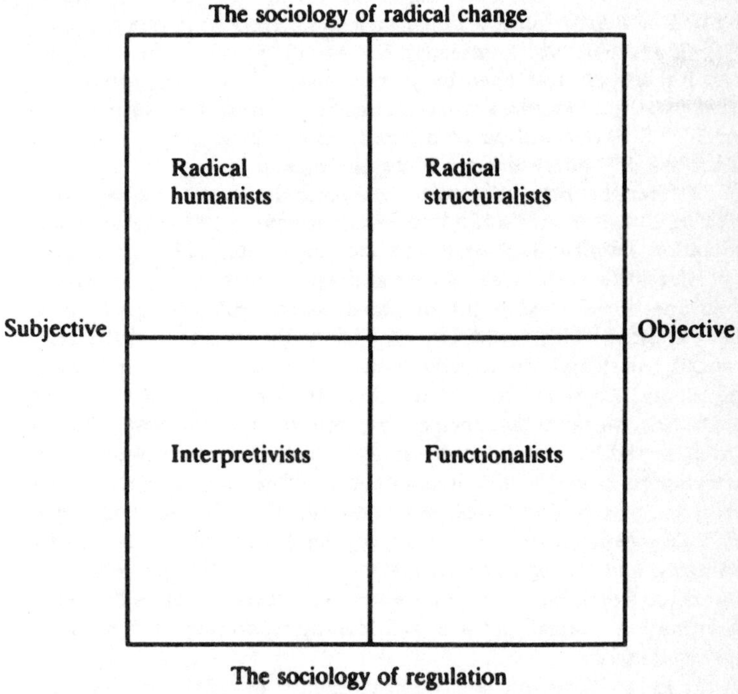

The sociology of radical change

|  |  |
|---|---|
| Radical humanists | Radical structuralists |
| Interpretivists | Functionalists |

Subjective ← → Objective

The sociology of regulation

*Figure 6.1*
*(after Burrell and Morgan 1979)*

As the authors explain (ibid., p.23), the diagram makes clear that each paradigm shares a common set of features with its neighbours on the horizontal and vertical axes in terms of one of the two dimensions but is differentiated on the other dimension:

> The four paradigms define fundamentally different perspectives for the analysis of social phenomena. They approach this endeavour from contrasting standpoints and generate quite different concepts and analytical tools (ibid., p.23).

It cannot be emphasized enough how important is this last statement. It cuts deep into social work thinking. Practitioners cannot tip-toe quietly by the assertion. The loud claim is that practice is saturated with theory no matter how much the social worker speaks of her simple reliance on commonsense or intuition. Each theory and its associated practice holds assumptions about people and their society which locate it within one of the four paradigms. Thus, in any piece of work, the problems perceived, explanations offered, the aims devised, and the methods used will vary fundamentally for each paradigm and its associated theories. In particular, there will be critical differences along one of the two major dimensions as we shift from one paradigm setting to another. Whittington and Holland (1985) also take advantage of the framework developed by Burrell and Morgan, identifying four parallel paradigms in social work that correspond to the four for social theory. Their work will be mentioned again a little later on but it is first necessary to note some recent developments.

Social theorists have continued to explore the nature of sociological theorizing. Johnson *et al* (1984) have taken issue with the rather static formulation implied in Burrell and Morgan's four major paradigms. They offer instead the idea of four strategies which emerge in answer to two questions: What is the nature of social reality? How is social reality known? This produces a potentially more sophisticated, historically alert and structurally dynamic approach to understanding social theory. Rojek (1986) makes note of the work of Johnson *et al* to remind social workers that theirs is a complex, fluid business which is not well served by particular theoretical camps constantly waging war and trying to capture and dominate the entire field of social work thought and action. Social work is just not like that. Stenson and Gould (1986) also express reservations about the framework presented by Whittington and Holland and ultimately Burrell and Morgan. They cite the work of Rojek and argue that social work theory has to be examined within a historical, political and ideological context before useful things can be said.

In the longer term this is an exciting line of thought, but there is a pressing short-term need to make solid headway into the mêlée of social work theory, especially as it is presented for practice. The Burrell and

Morgan paradigms provide a useful, well-equipped staging post on the way to understanding the nature and purpose of social work and its theories. It is true that there is a fascinating and intimate relationship between theories *for* social work and theories *of* social work. However, the distinctions, as well as connections, between these two sorts of theory is not always appreciated by analysts.

The nature of these relationships will again be alluded to in the final chapter, but I suspect that to develop such ideas requires a combination of intellectual skill, ambition and adventure that would be hard to handle without first laying some strong foundations. This takes us back to the paradigm staging post. Here the ground is reasonably solid. It gives us a chance to take bearings and see how the land of social work theory lies. When this is done, when we have mapped the terrain and learned how to describe the landscape, then we might dig beneath the surface, which is, of course, what all structuralists love to do.

### A taxonomy of social work theories

I have not used the nomenclature offered by Burrell and Morgan (or Whittington and Holland) to identify each paradigm, preferring instead to employ a racier set of chapter headings that hint at the four main orientations taken by social workers as they practise within the assumptions lying beneath each paradigm. The Burrell and Morgan titles are translated thus (also see Figure 6.2):

| | | |
|---|---|---|
| Functionalists | : | The fixers |
| Interpretivists | : | The seekers after meaning |
| Radical humanists | : | The raisers of consciousness |
| Radical structuralists | : | The revolutionaries |

These translations will not prevent mention of Burrell and Morgan's terminology, nor will they stop use being made of Whittington and Holland's excellent observations on the place of social work's theories in the framework.

### Social work theory and the structure of practice

In the subsequent chapters each paradigm receives a brief introduction. Next is added the book's other main organizing principle: that the process of practice should be clearly structured along the sequence:

1  Defining the problem.
2  Explanation and assessment.
3  Aims.
4  Methods.

When combined, these two organizing principles allow us to develop our oft claimed assertion that the theory held by a social worker fundamentally determines the character of her work at each stage of

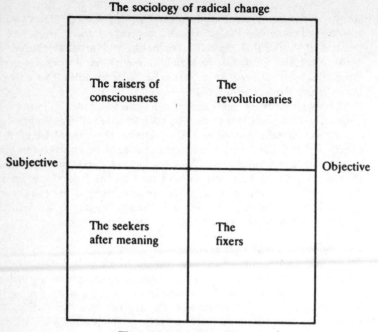

The sociology of radical change

| | |
|---|---|
| The raisers of consciousness | The revolutionaries |
| The seekers after meaning | The fixers |

Subjective — Objective

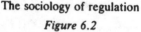

The sociology of regulation

*Figure 6.2*

the practice process. The paradigms are underpinned by a rationale that allows the social worker to choose her theories with an increased awareness of what each means for practice.

After the general introductory chapter for each paradigm, a particular social work theory and its practice is described, again using the organizing principles outlined above. Each theory serves as an example of thinking consistent with the assumptions of that paradigm. However, in the case of 'The fixers' (Chapter 7), two social work theories are given by way of example. The scale, variety and importance of practice within this orientation suggests that two examples, at least, would be required to convey something of the range to be found. Thus, social work in the psychoanalytical tradition (Chapter 8) and behavioural social work (Chapter 9) each receive a separate chapter.

'The seekers after meaning' (Chapter 10) offer an increasingly rich array of practices, but we shall confine ourselves to the client-centred approaches (Chapter 11) as a good illustration of the genre.

'The raisers of consciousness' (Chapter 12) are beginning to generate some extremely interesting pieces of work, spurred on in particular by feminist theory and writing. The example of radical social work (Chapter 13) describes the directions being pursued in this area.

'The revolutionaries' (Chapter 14) pose the biggest challenge to mainstream ideas about social work practice. I have referred to their practice as Marxist social work (Chapter 15) which is not altogether appropriate as areas of Marxism have also influenced the thinking of those who attempt to raise consciousness. Nevertheless, given the logic of the paradigms, theory and practice in this field is sufficiently distinct to warrant separate consideration.

The final chapter (16), 'Theories for social work and theories of social work', reviews the state of theorizing in social work and takes a tentative look into the future.

# 7 The Fixers

## Order and objective science

Theories located within the functionalist paradigm have two things in common: they are interested in the orderly relationships that exist between people; and they prefer to explore this interest in the style of the natural sciences. The functionalist is impressed by the regularity that exists in human affairs. The nature of such order, how it comes about and how it is maintained is the focus of their attention. There is an intriguing relationship between the behaviour of the conforming individual and the equilibrium exhibited by the social system as a whole.

If an individual's conduct does go astray, the functionalist keeps an eye on the social mechanisms employed to deal with such deviance and abnormality. By definition, 'anti-social' behaviour is understood to be 'pathological'. Being seen as such, it is eligible to be 'treated'. When cured, the individual can resume his normal place in society. There is a preparedness to apply such knowledge to help return the social system to equilibrium, to prevent disintegration. 'It is often problem-oriented in approach,' write Burrell and Morgan (1979, p.26), 'concerned to provide practical solutions to practical problems.' It is clear that the sociology of regulation, therefore, understands the term regulation in two ways. Firstly, the regular patterning of social life is recognized and applauded. Secondly, in order to maintain such stability, there is a need and preparedness to regulate and control behaviour.

Of course, some changes in social organization are necessary if equilibrium is to be held. For example, if the poorest members of society are too hard done by, they become restive. This would threaten social stability. Functionalists, therefore, are pragmatists, quite prepared to go in for modest social engineering. Resources should be redistributed to check any potentially destabilizing imbalances. Resources here may include money, opportunities and political rights. Reform is the preferred political strategy. Whenever the various parts of the social whole experience excessive strain, the system either automatically or through deliberate planning 'reforms' itself to relieve whatever pressures have been threatening stability and order.

The functionalist holds 'objectivist' views about the nature of social reality. That is to say, human nature is generally seen to be determined and not possessed of free will. Society and its people can be investigated from the standpoint of the independent observer. Explanations offered by the participants and the observed are not taken as acceptable accounts of what is actually going on. It is assumed that people, individually and collectively, are governed by rules and causal relationships. It is the job of the social scientist to identify these patterns of behaviour. The methods of enquiry are like those of the natural scientist. People show characteristics that can be understood and described objectively. The enquirer sets about individuals and their situations, intent on measuring, categorizing and establishing causal relationships.

The functionalist is also an empiricist, someone who takes the view that human activity is best approached as observable behaviour, behaviour that can be seen and described. The behaviour *is* what it is seen to be and no more. There is no need to look behind it for, if examined with stringency and accuracy, it will speak for itself if there are those with an ear to listen. If the social sciences are like the natural sciences, then behavioural and social knowledge is gained from what we see and sense directly. There is no reality beyond or beneath the reality observed. Hence, empiricists have little time for metaphysics and other philosophies, which query the material nature of reality. The empiricist believes that, by observing and describing the social world, an actual, independent reality is being captured and recorded. Any theory emanating from these observed facts can be tested against this independent reality. This suggests that the theorist's experience of the observed situation is neutral, influenced only by the independent reality itself. Causal relationships are assumed to exist between external behavioural and social events. If they can be plotted with sufficient clarity, behavioural and social laws can be identified.

Theoretically speaking, this is a densely populated paradigm. Many theories live under its influence which favours the objective examination of social order. Even so, there is great diversity and, perhaps more than any other, this paradigm has been home to a good many social theorists from sociology, psychology and anthropology. Crudely, and doing no justice to the sheer variety present, it is possible to recognize two broad types of functionalist theory: social systems; and behavioural. Both have spawned social work offspring.

### Social systems theory

The favourite analogies of structural functionalists and systems theorists are those of the biological organism (in the case of the former) and the complex machine (in the case of the latter). Essentially both recognize that different parts of a whole, functioning entity, such as society, the family or an individual body, are interrelated and interdependent. The performance of any one part not only affects other parts but may depend on those other parts for its survival and certainly the survival of the whole entity. This is why individual parts can be described as 'malfunctioning' and in need of 'repair', otherwise the whole system is threatened with breakdown. Similarly, it is possible to introduce change in one part of the system that produces change, either benign or malign, in another.

If the practitioner can analyze the system and the origin of its current malfunctioning, she can determine where to go for cure and change in order to bring about a new, stable and healthy equilibrium. For example, if the parents of a difficult adolescent can re-establish a less destructive marital relationship, it will have a positive effect on the behaviour of their teenage daughter.

Explaining the behaviour and function of individuals and institutions in this way has proved very attractive to social workers. The search for a theory which encompasses the individual as well as his social environment offered the prospect of a unified base to professional practice. Throughout the 1970s, 'systems theory', as has been seen, had a great impact on social work thinking. It gave rise to a number of significant publications including books by Pincus and Minahan (1973), Meyer (1976), Davies (1977), and Specht and Vickery (1977).

The most vigorous and least equivocal statement of mainstream theory and practice to emerge in recent years comes from Davies (1985) in *The Essential Social Worker: A Guide to Positive Practice*. Davies is an empiricist and a functionalist: it is his central argument 'that social work can only be understood by observing what it does and then by reflecting upon the contribution that these activities make to the way society ticks' (ibid., p.5). This leads him to develop his 'theory of maintenance'. Here, the social worker contributes:

> Towards the maintenance *of* society by exercising control over deviant members and allocating scarce resources according to policies laid down by the state but implemented on an individual basis. He is maintaining members *in* society by exercising control, by allocating resources and by the provision of a wide range of supportive strategies (ibid., p.30).

The result is a consensus model of practice, one in which the social worker functions to maintain society and its people in a relatively stable state. The book, true to its subtitle, guides the social worker through her work in a practical and positive, realistic and honest way, allowing Davies to assert, in what is perhaps the sentence most quoted from the book, that 'social workers are the maintenance mechanics oiling the interpersonal wheels of the community' (ibid., p.28).

### Behavioural theories
Whereas systems theories use the natural world as analogous to the social world, a technique which finds models useful for understanding

society, behaviourists 'treat the social world exactly as if it were the natural world; they treat human beings as machines or biological organisms, and social structure as if it were a physical structure' (Burrell and Morgan 1979, p.102).

In its most extreme form, people are treated just as any other natural organism, entirely determined by their biology and environment. The subjective dimension is deemed utterly irrelevant. Thoroughgoing behaviourists, for example, see no need whatsoever to consider notions such as human purpose, the unconscious and other 'speculative' and 'metaphysical' fancies in order to make sense of human behaviour. The social scientist seeks to understand how certain behaviours arise, how they persist and, if necessary, how they can be modified.

More generally, all theories that hope to identify universal psychological laws (the natural science end of the psychology spectrum) are operating on similar assumptions about the nature of people. Behavioural theory is the most scientifically rigorous in its style, but many Freudian-based psychologies are equally deterministic and scientific in their aspirations.

Social workers have shown a good deal of interest in scientifically inclined psychology. For over fifty years, psychoanalytic theories have influenced social workers. Their professional style matches many features of medical practice. Social workers *diagnose* problems and *treat* their clients. The social worker is the expert; she knows best. She knows what is the problem and how best it should be handled. Problem behaviour indicates a 'pathological' state which, if treated, may return the individual to 'healthy functioning'. Programmes of behaviour modification, problem-solving approaches based on post-Freudian ego-psychology and task-centred casework all have the idea that there is a faulty, problem behaviour to be spotted and that, if mended, the individual can resume normal, proper social functioning:

> The attraction of this general approach in social work is not difficult to understand. It demands of those who control the resources to social work that it shall demonstrate its effectiveness in changing the behaviour of the people who have 'problems', changes that can more easily be met by measuring externals rather than in any other way. Economical, tough-minded, and 'hard-scientific' explanations come as something of a relief in social work after so many years of convoluted, tender-minded and woolly explanations (Leonard 1975, p.328).

As has been said, there is an enormous range of theory to be found within the paradigm. Yet the basic assumptions about human nature, the methods best suited to the study of people and their society as well as the nature of that society vary little across different 'functionalist' theories.

Throughout the following sections on the social work process, it is still necessary to retain the division between behavioural and systems theories. Although both recognize pathological states, the level at which the malfunction is identified varies. Whereas behavioural theories locate difficulties within the individual, systems theorists consider the effect the whole system has on the problem part. Both theories seek to return things to their proper functioning and a state of equilibrium, but the locus of intervention differs.

**Defining the problem: people with problems and people as problems**
'The paradigm allows that some social problems have structural roots,' suggest Whittington and Holland (1985, p.35), 'but emphasises that many others arise from misfortune, human tragedy and personal inadequacy.' Indeed, in many theoretical stances, the cause of problems is clearly identified as an individual pathology, often psychological in origin. Moving into more sociological territory, incomplete socialization is defined as a problem. 'Thus,' continue Whittington and Holland:

> Failure to perform the roles of pupil, employer [sic], spouse, parent or responsible, law-abiding citizen may be seen as the result of defects in the process of learning and internalising the necessary rules, values, skills and forms of conduct (ibid., p.36).

So the world of social work clients is divided into those who *have* problems and those who *are* problems.

However, it is also possible to look at problems in terms of the proper functioning of a system. Rather than see an individual having a problem in isolation, the problem can be considered as a property of the whole system. Relationships between the parts of a system may place strains and stresses on an individual unit as it experiences demands from the rest of the system. For example, an apparently innocuous reduction in the frequency of rent collections by the Housing Department in an attempt to save money (regarded as a good idea) has the unintended effect of increasing the number of tenants who fall into serious rent arrears. Only after a rapid rise in the number of threatened evictions does it become clear that weekly wage earners and those on state benefits do not lead life styles that allow large sums of cash to accrue in order to pay a hefty monthly rent.

Family therapists have been enthusiastic users of systems theory. Many of them prefer to treat all members as part of a whole functioning family system. Behaviour in one part of the system, say tension in the marriage, may affect behaviour elsewhere in the system, say a child becoming withdrawn and unresponsive. The two sub-units of the system have to be considered within the context of the functioning whole. Rather than talk of 'sick' individuals, the family therapist prefers to think in terms of maladaptive family processes.

**Explanation and assessment: diagnosis and rational analysis**

The assessment phase seeks to identify where the system is malfunctioning or what is causing the unacceptable behaviour. The practitioner looks for what is going wrong. She seeks an objective account of what is causing the problem behaviour. To help her do this, she observes, gathers facts and acquires information. This enables her to make a diagnosis of what is wrong and explain what is causing it. Having diagnosed the problem, she can then prescribe a course of treatment — things to be done if the problem condition is to be cured.

The explanation may be shared with the client (as behaviourists do) or the client may be helped to appreciate the expert's explanation as he gains 'insight' into his difficulties (which is what Freudians encourage). However, in both cases, it is the worker who holds the explanation. She remains the expert in understanding what is going on and this she may or may not divulge to the client.

The systems theorist, or systems analyst as we call her in this section, sees inappropriate system functioning as the cause of individual troubles. 'Social systems theory,' writes Whittaker (1974, p.89), 'deals with the way in which various social systems such as families, small groups, organisations, communities and societies are created and . . . maintained or changed.' Social workers learn to work out how different parts of the system relate to each other and how the behaviour of one part will affect the performance of another. For instance, an assessment may be much more worthwhile when it recognizes the effect of disbanding the local playgroup which, coupled with the absence of any nearby day nursery, adversely affects the lives of mothers at home in high-rise flats with young children. Not only does this map out a more likely explanation of their depressed state of mind, it also suggests that it is the larger resource and service system that has to be the target for change and not the psyches of the stress-ridden mothers.

**Aims: mend and maintain**

Essentially, the aim in each case is to recover the individual or the social system to proper, healthy and harmonious functioning. It is bad for both the individual and the overall wellbeing of society for them to be out of sorts with each other. This can be appreciated in the following examples.

A young mother's skills in caring for her baby are assessed as weak and possibly harmful. The aim is to improve her performance as a parent and, in so doing, to reduce the risk to the child. Another example is that of working with an offender, aiming to stop him committing further crimes. Aiming to change the policy of the Housing Department will help break up the ghettos in which are concentrated tenants with severe rent arrears, low morale and criminal propensities. The present effect on the estate's children is very damaging. Poor socialization causes them to misbehave and become a social problem.

Not surprisingly, the aims of the systems theorist are to restore the system to proper working order. Systems that malfunction, whether families, groups or communities, are inefficient, ineffective and liable to disintegrate, with great social cost. The prevention of such break-downs is the goal of the systems theorist.

Functionalist aims always start with phrases such as 'to stop him committing further offences . . .', 'to improve her social functioning . . .', 'to improve her child-rearing abilities . . .', 'to cure him of his drink problem . . .'.

## Methods: treatment, support and maintenance

Although the techniques employed range from rewarding desired behaviours through to encouraging insight into the emotional origins of one's feckless ways, the methods all seek to help the individual change so that he lives more acceptably in his social environment.

In all theoretical schools, the practitioner is the expert. She is the one who identifies the faulty part. She applies her objective knowledge and expertise to fix it. She is responsible for saying what should be done. As a scientist, the social worker knows how people work. She explains how circumstances cause problems. Whereas the car mechanic recommends replacing dirty sparking plugs, the social worker advises a mother to respond more demonstratively and affectionately to her difficult daughter. While the nutritionist prescribes a course of lemons for the patient with scurvy, the social worker tells an unhappy wife to buy some new clothes and be sexually more forthcoming if she wants to revive a flagging marriage.

In the case of the systems theorist, the explanation of how a system operates provides clear clues about what has to be fixed if a mal-function occurs. We have already said that a change in one part of the system may bring about a change either in the system as a whole or in a part elsewhere in that whole system.

Social workers often facilitate improvements in a system by oiling the works. They mediate between different parts. They clear communication channels that have become blocked so that all parts can be aware of what is going on. Workers carry pieces of information from one group to another. For example, in a hospital ward, if patients and doctors do not communicate accurately with one another, information germane to the system's basic purpose is lost. Communications failure upsets effective system functioning. Foster (in Pincus and Minahan 1973, pp.300–8) reminds us that, in most medical settings, helping patients and their families cope with the problems arising from illness actually facilitates recovery or, in the case of the terminally ill, allows those involved to come to terms with and explore the implications of impending death. In the case she describes, communication between doctors and patients was woefully inadequate. Information was not free-flowing. Patients, although they had their suspicions, were not put fully in the picture. The social worker intervened in the system. She listened to the feelings and ideas of the patients and reported them to the doctors and nurses. It was clear that if patients were to cope with their serious condition their feelings had to be understood. They had to become part of the decision-making process which affected *their* lives. Through mediation, by opening blocked channels of communication and by altering the assumptions held by different parts of the ward system, the worker brought about basic improvements in a critical field of the hospital's functioning.

## Conclusion

Social work which is about treating people and situations has been served by a number of theories. I have already mentioned systems theory and the integrated methods school, but shall rest them at this stage. I have chosen psychoanalysis and behaviourism as the two theories which I think best illustrate how thinking affects practice in this paradigm.

The psychoanalytic tradition in social work has been long, fine and impossible to ignore. Even though its heyday may have passed, much of its wisdom has entered social work's soul and we are not always aware of its pervasive legacy.

Behavioural social work, though, is still in the ascendancy. For those who believe that social workers should be like doctors and that doctors are people who use science, then science is for social workers. The only candidate with really strong scientific credentials is behavioural social work. If social workers want to be effective they have to find effective cures. The rigorous and exacting methods of science will help social workers identify treatment procedures that lead to behavioural cures.

In 1980, Brewer and Lait savaged social workers for their ineffectiveness. Other theoretical outlooks will have things to say about whether curing the pathological state of individuals is really anything to do with social work or even a proper way to view welfare matters. However, Brewer and Lait recommend social workers to become scientists if they want to survive as an occupational group. 'Become a behaviourist' is their specific advice. Only the behaviourist possesses scientific objectivity, which is the true road to effectiveness. Chapter 9 outlines the theory and practice of behavioural social work. Before that, however, let us consider Freud and his followers.

# 8 The Psychoanalytic Tradition in Social Work

Freudian psychology has long held attractions for social workers. Historically it was the earliest psychological theory to interest social workers. As far back as 1918 Freudian psychology was taught at Smith College Training School for Psychiatric Social Work in the United States. Not only was it the first psychological theory, for fifty years it was also the most influential (Yelloly 1980). This makes any potted version of Freud and social work extremely difficult to achieve. His ideas permeated social work writing for several decades. Moreover, Freud stands as a major intellectual figure whose thoughts have revolutionized much of the way we think about ourselves and other people. Nor has his psychology stood still. Not only did he continually modify his own ideas, but during his lifetime and since his death all kinds of variants and developments have emerged including ego-psychology, object-relations theory and existential psychoanalysis. Together these theorists are known as the post-Freudians. The work of people such as Melanie Klein, John Bowlby and David Winnicott has been particularly influential on social work practice.

A fairly classic rendition of both the underlying psychology and the use made of it by social workers will be offered here. Its scientific and functionalist qualities will be recognized. These require the social worker to make objective diagnoses of other people's behaviour. A cure is then attempted through a course of treatment. Although psychoanalytic-styled casework has gone largely out of fashion, it still evinces strong support in many quarters. For example, Butrym (1981) makes out a good case for social workers understanding the nature of defence mechanisms and the centrality of dependence in personal relationships. Stalwarts of traditional practices have banded together to form the 'Group for the Advancement of Psychodynamics and Psychotherapy in Social Work'. In the mid-1980s this group launched a new twice-yearly publication, the *Journal of Social Work Practice*, carrying papers with a strong psychodynamic and analytical flavour.

In its later developments psychodynamic thinking has shed tremendous light on the relationship between the social worker and her client (Saltzberger-Wittenberg 1970; Ferard and Hunnybun 1962). The importance of the 'relationship' received an eloquent boost in the work of Mattinson and Sinclair (1979). They practised marital casework, using psychoanalytically derived principles, with the parents of families referred to a Social Services Department. The work is reported in *Mate and Stalemate* (1979), a fascinating account of how Bowlby's theory of attachment and loss informed the practice of marital work in a non-clinical setting. They seek to demonstrate that establishing a therapeutic relationship along modern psychoanalytic lines is highly relevant to the 'hurly-burly' of a social services area team.

The intention of this chapter is not to give a thoroughly up-to-date review of all the developments, varieties and off-shoots of Freudian-derived practices, of which there are many. What will be done is to remain true to our theme and see how the basic assumptions of a Freudian psychology guide the style and content of the social work process. In particular we shall learn how past childhood experiences have a critical bearing on current behaviour, we shall appreciate that behavioural symptoms are the surface manifestation of deeper inner psychic states and we shall know that in order to change behaviour we have to treat the individual's inner psychological condition.

Four basic concepts are welded into Freud's psychoanalytical thought: determinism, the instincts and drives, the psychosexual stages of development, and unconscious mental states. We shall consider each of these as they help us to think about the ways problems arise and how they might be explained.

### Determinism

Freud saw himself as a scientist. He was born in 1856 and when still quite young he moved to Vienna with his family. At the University of Vienna Freud first studied physiology and biology before pursuing a medical degree. According to Freud, our behaviour, including what we say, do and think, is 'caused' very often by experiences, memories and needs, many of which we are not consciously aware. Even apparently minor behaviours such as slips of the tongue indicate deeper determining causes which reveal the true state of our mind. We are and we remain irredeemably biological organisms, subject to the full power of nature and our instincts.

Further confirmation of the scientific character of psychoanalysis is given by its 'reductionist' tendencies. This proceeds on the basis that men, women and their personalities can be reduced to a limited number of constituent features. Human beings are no more than the sum of these biological and psychological mechanisms. The instincts, in particular, exert a strong control over our behaviour. At root, behaviour is understood in terms of attempts to satisfy basic, innate needs and not as an example of free choice. This presents a pessimistic view of human nature in so far as behaviour is seen to be no more than a complex manifestation of biological drives that have to be controlled, checked and channelled in human society.

## The basic drives: sex and aggression

Instincts drive the individual through his or her life. They mobilize the human organism into activity. This is biologically necessary if the organism is to do two fundamentally important things: survive and reproduce. Or put another way, we all have to set about the world if we are to maintain ourselves physically and we are compelled into sexual behaviour if we favour perpetuating the species. As will be seen, how we handle all this potent stuff has a marked bearing on the kind of person we turn out to be.

Physiological needs cause tensions in the body. These states of excitement cannot go unheeded if life is to be maintained. They are also experienced by that part of the central nervous system called the mind. These instincts are represented mentally in terms of wishes, which are turned towards objects and people for their satisfaction. In this way the mind receives its psychic energy or excitation. The mind is now in a position to direct the body (through action of all kinds including words as well as deeds) to do something about the needs which it experiences. Thus we have states of psychic excitement known as the basic drives, which are a direct mental response to the demands of the body. The activity that results from these bodily tensions and high energy psychic states lead the individual to seek ways of gratifying the needs and reducing the tension. As we try to gratify these needs in a social context, the presence and reactions of other people adds yet another factor that we have to consider and handle.

Two basic drives can be identified: the sexual, and the aggressive. In a broader sense, these drives can be seen as a general requirement if any body is to persist. Freud certainly saw, for example, the sex drive as more than just the urge to reproduce, and he believed the aggressive instincts were more than simple gratuitous acts of violence or bad temper. In order to live, we have to 'get at' our environment. We have to be curious and inquisitive about what is around us in order to find what we need. We must seek out, obtain and control the things necessary for life. These require an aggressive, probing attitude to the environment. Once we have come across the things which are necessary for living, the next task is to use them, incorporate them and absorb them. So whether it is eating, uniting for sexual purposes or possessing things so that they might be used, the sensation is physically pleasurable which, in its broad sense, is to say sexual. The psychic counterpart of this sexual energy is called the libido.

Both drives are often fused in our thoughts and acts. Aggressive behaviour can have a pleasurable component. We bite, eat and relish the taste of food. Sexual intercourse involves penetration and incorporation. To touch and be touched can provide mutual pleasure.

## Psychosexual development

Freud went on to say that the drives were not only pervasive through-out all aspects of adult human behaviour but they were present in children from birth onwards. This did not go down too well with the Victorians. The claim was that the way the developing child experi-enced and learned to handle his or her libido and aggressive instincts was fundamental to the type of personality that developed. Psycho-analysis asserts that the adult character is a direct result of early childhood experiences. In particular, the first five years are a critical time in which the individual's personality is laid down. There are three stages of psychosexual development through which the child grows. If adults and their behaviour are to be understood properly, it is crucial that the potential twists and turns of each of these stages is fully appreciated.

Each stage is distinguished on the basis of the zone of the body through which the drives are being manifested. These are known as the 'erogenous zones'. They are places where pleasurable sensations might be experienced. As the infant develops and the child gradually acquires control over key areas of functioning, we see a shift in the site of these erogenous zones from the mouth to the anus and eventually to the genitals. These promote three major stages of psychosexual develop-ment: the oral, the anal and the phallic-urethral or genital.

The first phase, the oral, occurs between birth and about eighteen months. Sucking and biting witness the erotic and aggressive instincts acting to help the baby find food and take it in. After these first eighteen months, the pleasurable area shifts to the anus. Sensing and controlling the processes of elimination and retention become critical at this stage. Between the ages of three and five, the focus moves on to the penis in boys and the clitoris in girls. Together these comprise the genital stage, characterized by the pleasure derived from manipulation and penetration.

What must be appreciated is that each stage has to be worked out by the infant with reference to the actions and reactions of other people. 'Other people' usually means the child's parents or caretakers. The style and quality of parenting received by the child is fundamentally important to the eventual character of the adult: 'the child is father to the man'. Thus, the first relationships are the most significant because they coincide with the infant's early stages of psychological development which occur at a time when he or she is physically and psychologically highly dependent on the efforts of the caring adults. Should these relationships be inadequate, faulty or unsatisfactory, psychological development is impaired.

At each of these stages the child is faced with conflicts between instinctual desires and the conscious activities of the mind. The manner in which the child deals with such conflicts was thought

by Freud to have a profound influence on the future development of his/her personality. Stages where instinctual desire are
either completely frustrated or too readily gratified may become
points of 'fixation' in the development of personality, points to
which the adult may well return if confronted by intolerable
stresses in later life (Fonagy and Higgitt 1984, p.28).

The successful resolution of frustrations and conflicts encountered
at each psychosexual stage results in normal, healthy development.
The adult personality shows no disturbed behavioural tendencies. In
those who are psychologically stable, there is no distortion of reality,
no resort to the psychically primitive devices used by infants in the
face of tension and anxiety.

When there are problems in psychosexual development, Freudian
theory suggests that the individual's personality will display certain,
highly characteristic pathological traits. Each personality trait can be
considered in terms of the psychosexual stage in which that particular
type of conflict or frustration first occurred. Psychologically, the
individual operates at the level at which development ran into
difficulties. He or she is said to be 'fixated' at a particular stage of
psychosexual development and so may be described as an oral, anal or
phallic character. As these 'character disorders' underlie so much of the
diagnostic focus of Freudian-based casework, it is necessary to examine
each stage in more detail and see what kind of characters they spawn
when the developmental experiences of children hit rough times.

## The character disordered personality

It is now clear that psychoanalytic theory suggests that people who
have not succeeded in progressing through the early stages of emotional
development are liable to display immature and childish behaviour.
They are prone to be impulsive. They form a major part of the clientèle
of any social work agency. Often they are described as 'problem
families' and it is quite usual for them to be on the agency's 'books' for
years on end. Such clients are said to be emotionally 'fixated' at
infantile levels of personality development. They are very susceptible
to emotional conflicts and they express these conflicts in their
behaviour. 'Acting-out' rather than 'thinking-through' is the usual
reaction to worries and upsets of which there are likely to be many.

These clients are still trying to resolve early infantile conflicts when
they failed to feel or to receive regular or consistent care. It was at
these early stages that the individual failed to learn how to handle
emotional stress, a failure that haunts them into adult life leaving them
vulnerable and doomed to repeat their primitive emotional responses
unless treated. Crises and problems dog their days. Impending evictions,
unplanned pregnancies, acts of delinquency, disputes with relatives,
rows with neighbours, shortage of money and a proneness to accidents

seem to characterize the lives of these clients. They communicate through their behaviour and so it is their behaviour that has to be understood and interpreted. It is not a matter of intelligence. Many such clients may well have strong intellects. It is simply a case of emotional immaturity.

The childhood of these clients appears to have been one in which neglect, disinterest or inconsistency on the part of the parent has been so evident that the child experienced a series of traumatic episodes. They behave as if they have been abandoned at some critical stage in their emotional development. This results in certain traits that are characteristic of the stage at which they felt 'abandoned', literally or emotionally. The child experiencing this trauma attempts to reduce the ensuing anxiety and tension. The child's only 'weapon' is his or her own body, what he or she does with it. This in turn is determined by where the child is up to in his or her psychosexual development. This results in characters which too can be described as oral, anal or phallic.

### The oral character

During the first eighteen months, the baby shows an innate ability to 'take in' by the mouth, itself part of a general approach to the world best described as 'incorporation'. The baby 'takes in' not only with the mouth, but with eyes, hands and all the senses. If the environment (particularly the mother) is in tune with this oral approach, the baby will develop a sense of security and general wellbeing. However, if these basic oral needs are upset, disrupted or lost through some parental failure, emotional development is impaired. The baby can no longer trust the world to be reliable. The baby, and its adult equivalent, gets what it can, while it can and holds on to it.

The prevailing wisdom is that social work agencies are replete with clients possessing oral personalities. They are impulsive. They are inclined to buy extravagant and unnecessary things. Although the electricity is about to be disconnected, a microwave oven, bought on hire purchase, suddenly appears. They are impatient for gratification. Walking home from the DHSS, a large mother and her large brood may be seen eating crisps, ice-creams and cakes though there is no other food in the house. Orally fixated mothers treat their children as 'a part of themselves'. The children hear all about mum's problems over money, sex and squabbles. She has a sibling-type relationship with her offspring. Mother and children are always together, going around as a noisy group to the welfare, to the clinic, to the shops. There is a 'nest-like' quality to home life. The children may well sleep with their mother in the same large double bed. Relationships are 'incorporative' because the personality has not succeeded in separating itself from others, a situation normally achieved between a mother and child at this stage. Social workers are encouraged to become 'part of the family': 'Jane, our social worker, is ever so nice, just like one of the family. She often pops in to join us for a sit down and a cup of tea.'

Dependency on others is another characteristic. If you express concern and show competence, you are that mother who might offer security and comfort. However, such demanding dependency is wearing. The insatiable needs of the oral character test the most giving of neighbours, the most patient of social workers. Vigorous rejection is often the only way out for the drained mother-figure and in this the client is simply repeating and confirming the original oral loss and perpetuating her emotional weakness. To trust others is fraught with danger and potential hurt. It is safer to mistrust and get what you can while you can. This, of course, brings about further rejection. The oral personality recognizes only two sorts of people (two sorts of social worker): those who are for her (part of her), and those who are against her (outside her).

Two kinds of oral character are identifiable. The first is associated with the earlier phase of sucking (the oral-erotic character). The second corresponds to the slightly later phase of biting (the oral-sadistic character).

The oral-erotic personality initially received a reasonable amount of milk, breast and attention, but then lost them. They are the sucking, seeking clients who expect and need attention. Their felt loss is filled with food or drink, money or sex. There may be problems of obesity. Promiscuity is common, not for sex, but as a restless search for closeness. They crave affection, but fear it hurting them again when it is withdrawn. Babies, pets and cuddly toys are safe though. Such things are wholly dependent, but, when babies grow up and show independence, they may be rejected or provoke feelings of helplessness and anxiety. The search for immediate gratification means that life is never dull. Things are always happening. Crises abound. Drama is the order of each day. They are well known to health visitors, doctors and social workers alike.

The oral-sadistic personality is associated with weaning. There is a tendency to 'bite', to take and hold on to things. Breasts are inclined to disappear when bitten by teething babies. This leads to confusion: the oral pleasure of biting sometimes leads to the removal of the thing desired. Such personalities are wary of others and what they offer. They have little to give themselves, but will snatch what they can from relationships. Unlike the oral-erotic character, they keep their demanding children at a physical and emotional distance. The oral-sadistic personality will complain a great deal, ask a great deal but never be satisfied.

## The anal character

Issues arising between the first and third years of life centre around the growing need to achieve some control over one's self. Bowel control and potty training are the focus of infant pleasure and parental concern. When muscles develop there is the potential to increase self-control. There is a capacity physically, and then psychically, to withhold and to expel. To lose control is to lose love which provokes anxiety. Love is conditional. If you do this for me, then, and only then, will I do something for you. The bargains struck at the time of potty training are echoed in later relationships. Whereas the child is self-centred and feels omnipotent in the oral stage, the child in the anal stage credits the parent with all the power. The child has to conform to the wishes of the parent if love is to be received. However, the child is also capable of manipulating relationships: to give only if he or she receives.

The anal phase is subject to the contradictory impulses of retention and elimination. Socially this is expressed in issues of 'letting go' and 'holding on'. The infant struggles for autonomy, with stubbornness looming large. Conflicts over giving and taking are commonplace. Anal characters tend to be either in tight self-control or completely messy. Fastidiousness, concern over order, punctuality and working to a routine suggest the individual is spending a lot of energy on anal matters.

Reflecting the contrasts between holding and letting go, and giving only if there is a promise of receiving, anal characters see things in black and white terms. Things are either right or wrong, strong or weak. There is a general fear of impulses and strong emotions as things potentially uncontrollable. Feelings are kept in check, though one suspects they rage beneath the surface. When they do let go, all hell lets loose. In order to win affection and regard, the anal personality shows an exaggerated compliance with the wishes of others but with the definite expectation of some reward. If this is not forthcoming, anger or depression (anger which is turned inwards) is the result.

Anal types have problems admitting weakness or becoming dependent. They insist on being seen as strong, independent and in control. However, this makes them vulnerable to set-backs. Again, the only reactions available to the anal type are either wild anger or depression. Inevitably they seek to control their own children, wanting to know what they are doing or thinking. With teenagers this is a recipe for conflict. Any assertion of independence on the part of the child is read as 'getting out of control': someone must do something about it. To the outsider things never appear as bad or as messy as they do to the anal parent. For him or her, what cannot be controlled has to be abandoned.

### The phallic character
Between three and five years, the child shows more assertiveness. There

is greater initiative. The child is curious about the world around. Infantile genitality is expressed by acts which are either 'intrusive' (being physically boisterous, talking in a deliberately challenging and provocative manner, showing simple curiosity, being competitive) or 'inclusive' (being motherly or taking on a parental role through play).

This is also the time of the Oedipus complex. Here the boy's sexual feelings for his mother, coupled with the fear of his father (castration anxieties), who is seen as a more powerful rival, are normally resolved by the boy eventually identifying with the father and so repressing any interest in his mother. Freud never really got to grips with female sexuality, but the fear of retribution is less intense in girls than boys, with the result that Oedipal attitudes are less strongly repressed in women with fathers frequently remaining a sexually attractive figure.

Various parental failures are possible at this stage. Any skewed or imbalanced marital relationship confuses the child who may not be able to resolve the Oedipal conflict. So when fathers are weak and mothers overbearing, or the sex roles unclear, processes of identification and repression go astray. Children who experience such parenting are liable to be bossy though in fact they remain fragile underneath and crumble under pressure. Competitiveness is another characteristic. There is a constant need to be in front, whether at work or in relationships. Although fixations at this level do produce these emotional weaknesses, they are not as socially debilitating as those associated with the oral and anal character types. In fact in some walks of life they may bring advantages. Accordingly, the phallic personality is rarely seen in welfare agencies, at least not amongst the clientèle.

## The unconscious and structures of the mind

Freud postulated that there are unconscious mental states. There is more to the mind than that of which we are immediately aware or can consciously bring to mind. Beneath the surface consciousness of the mind lies a deeper layer of unconscious activity. It is dominated by the mental representations of the desires and impulses that any organism experiences in order to live.

Over the years, Freud gradually refined his models of the mind and eventually produced a three-part structure representing the various layers of mental activity:

1 The id, which contains all the instinctual drives and which operates on the pleasure principle.
2 The ego, which deals with the real world outside.
3 The super-ego, which is a specialized part of the ego advocating constraint, showing a social conscience and possessing ideals.

According to Freud, the ego and super-ego develop slowly out of the id in the child's early years of life.

## The id

This gives psychic expression to the body's needs. It pays no heed to reality, only to the basic biological demands of the organism which, if it is to continue in existence, must be met. The id cannot tolerate increases in its energy without suffering tension. The body's demands for food, warmth and relief from pain cause the id to operate solely on the pleasure principle. It has no sense of right or wrong, what is practical or reasonable. It demands immediate satisfaction. As such this part of the psyche is selfish, restless, unprincipled, a veritable cauldron of needs and desires. The id itself is not capable of organizing the individual to have these instinctual demands met, but, by bringing them forcibly into the mind, they are hard to ignore. In the case of the baby who can only cry and thrash about when it is hungry or cold, it has to rely on others to help reduce these instinctual demands and so relieve psychic tension. We see that the way other people help the infant cope with these demands is critical to the levels of anxiety and tension that the baby experiences and with which it has to cope. The id, then, is the reservoir of all psychic energy, the locus of sexual and aggressive drives. It is the very stuff of life.

## The ego

As far as the individual is concerned, the insistent demands of the id do two things. Firstly, they bring the person into contact with the outside world where he or she needs to be if physiological demands are to be met. Secondly, the id requires the individual to interact with this world in order to obtain the things that are needed to appease the pressing demands of the id. In doing these things, the developing individual both learns about the world and increasingly appreciates that it is necessary to consider the external environment in a more calculating, circumspect and realistic way if survival is to be achieved. The world tends not to jump to the id's demands. Parents do not immediately satisfy a baby's every need.

It is those parts of the psyche which rub against the outside world, and which are obliged to consider it, that gradually evolve into the ego. Freud suggested that even when the ego was being more realistic than the id, nevertheless it was still bent on achieving instinctual gratification. The ego is, therefore, an executant of the instinctual drives. Whereas the id knows only its own condition, the ego considers both internal demands (id) and external constraints (reality).

In order to achieve a balance between the body, its needs and the hazards involved in exploiting the environment, the ego has to consider and eventually control:

- The body's motor functions (to move about and get at the world).
- The body's perceptual organs (to obtain information about the world).

- The memory (to recall experiences of the world and remember lessons learned).
- Thought processes (to evaluate and calculate the best course of action between the instincts and how they are to be satisfied).

These abilities make up the ego. Whereas the id operates on the un-bridled pleasure principle, the ego computes on the reality principle. The resultant 'manifest' behaviour is the end-product of these various 'dynamic' forces, each pulling in their own preferred direction. This is why psychoanalytic work is often referred to as psychodynamic.

Generally, with increased experience of the environment, the ego continues to grow and strengthen. Slowly a sense of reality develops. At first, the infant cannot distinguish between its own body sensations and those from the environment. This changes with experience. Frustration, in moderation, is necessary for ego development. The baby needs to sense that there is a world out there. If the infant yells for food and nothing happens, this is a sharp reminder that there are things outside his or her control. There is a world beyond the body that does not always do what the baby wants. This is a lesson it will have to learn quickly if it is to survive, become independent and live successfully. A totally indulgent parent who panders to an infant's every desire denies that child the chance of developing a strong ego. The id remains to the fore and so we have the spoilt child, who demands and screams until he or she has his or her own way. No one has helped such a child cope with the world directly or independently. 'An intact reality sense enables the ego to act efficiently upon the environment in the interests of the id' (Brenner 1955, p.72). Those whose egos are weak have an unrealistic view of the world. They easily feel out of control. When frustrated, the fragile ego acts in ways that are essentially infantile. This brings us back to the psychosexual development of the infant.

In order for the ego to acquire self-control and gain realistic experiences of the world (for example, delaying gratification without throwing a tantrum), the baby needs an initially sympathetic and 'good-enough' environment which, in effect, acts as the infant's ego. Mothers who keep at bay too much unmanageable tension are behaving rather like an ego, sensitive to what is happening and to what is wanted on the baby's behalf.

However, not all mothers are 'good-enough' (John Bowlby). Some neglect, others disappear. Certainly, brief periods of frustration, as has been seen, are not only tolerable but necessary for the ego to emerge. It is only when frustrations become too much that the psyche is over-whelmed (a trauma), threatening satisfactory emotional development. We have heard what happens in such instances. Depending on the psychosexual stage reached, particular fixations and their associated character traits will result. The quality of the caring environment is crucial to the type of personality that emerges. The terrible irony is that the failures of parents to provide a reasonably consistent, anxiety-free environment produce a weak ego. Fragile egos are thrown by the normal ups and downs of everyday life. The world is experienced as inconsistent, hostile and a source of anxiety. Mature mechanisms for handling anxiety are absent and so the individual resorts to infantile emotional responses: the fixations met in the oral, anal and phallic personalities.

## The super-ego

As the child continues to grow and develop, it experiences parents as people who impose order and set boundaries to what can and cannot be done in the family and in society. The super-ego is the psychic representation of the parental authority figures. These figures become internalized in a version which is simpler, sterner and less tolerant than the real thing. The super-ego contains the conscience. It worries about what is socially expected. It is a source of guilt as it monitors what the id and the ego are up to as they seek to get what they can from the world around.

## Anxiety and the defence mechanisms

Anything that threatens the ego's integrity is likely to cause anxiety. Anxiety is experienced both physically and psychically. The function it serves is to warn the ego that there is danger. This danger can come from the unmet needs of the body as portrayed by the id. Or it can come in the form of external dangers as the environment reacts to the pressing demands of the id. If the anxiety level is too high, a 'trauma' is experienced by the ego as it loses control. Hollis (1964) is in no doubt that anxiety is something to which the social worker must be extra sensitive:

> No single factor in treatment is more important than the worker's keeping his finger on the pulse of the client's anxiety . . . What particular things in the client's present or past provoke his anxiousness? How does his anxiety show itself and how does he handle it? In particular: does his anxiety level impel him to unwise acting out? Does it result in increased neurotic or somatic symptomatology? What defenses does he use against it? Is he immobilised? Will he run away from treatment? (p.315).

People often distort reality in ways which, given the circumstances, do not appear to make sense. They may over-react to seemingly innocuous statements, they may respond with anger to someone who appears to have behaved quite reasonably, they may deny an important factor in their situation which seems patently relevant to the outsider. In these cases it may be suggested that a psychological defence mechanism is in operation. It is a way of dealing with anxiety and warding off pain. When challenged, the person with the defence will rarely admit to its use.

Defence mechanisms are those unconscious strategies designed to protect the individual from pain, anxiety and guilt which cannot be handled in real-world terms. Defences arise as a reasonable response to unreasonable circumstances, but they remain, ultimately, weak and immature behaviours. They frustrate growth and learning. They perpetuate the ego's weakness in the face of difficult situations. The true nature of the anxiety is masked. Reality is fudged.

Conflict, which brings anxiety in its wake, stems from three sources. Firstly there are the demands of the external world – other people, material objects, social reactions. Secondly there is pressure from the internal drives of sex and aggression pushing up through the id. Thirdly there are the curbs set by the super-ego, constantly reminding the ego that this behaviour is not socially acceptable or that action is not the sort of thing a person like you should do. It is a function of the ego to mediate between these demands, but, when a compromise is not possible, the ego resorts to defensive behaviour. The conflict is distorted or repressed in such a way that the situation becomes temporarily tolerable. However, the real issue has been avoided and will recur. This is when the student of defence mechanisms hears George Santayana's famous words: 'Those who cannot remember the past are condemned to repeat it.'

There are many defence mechanisms. Most of us use some of them at one time or another in situations that we cannot quite handle, or admit to be unable to handle. We may simply avoid them, providing ourselves with personally convincing excuses. The defence of 'intellectualization' is seen when a person, who cannot respond to the strong feelings being aroused, chooses instead to consider matters in an abstract, theoretical, dispassionate way as if they were really nothing to do with that person but just happen to be a subject of passing academic interest.

'Projection' is a commonly used defence. Here, we attribute to someone else our own unwanted impulses and then react to that person in the light of those very feelings which we have projected on to them. We treat them for what we are. So, if I have had a bad day it is never me that is angry but you. I am only reacting to your temper. In truth, of course, the other becomes angry in response to the initial, unfair accusation. Nevertheless, once the other has become heated, it confirms the original accusation. The projectionist brings about the very situation which she alleges.

In 'reaction-formations', anxiety-provoking impulses are heavily suppressed, so much so that the person behaves in a way completely opposite to that of the underlying instinct. Men who rail against homosexuals with apoplectic vehemence, and who cannot stop talking about the rampant decadence of single sex relationships, very often mask great uncertainties about their own heterosexuality.

There are many other defences which receive full treatment in the literature, but, for the interested reader, the seminal work of Anna Freud (1936), Sigmund's youngest daughter, is still a sound point at which to start.

## Freudian aetiology and its implications for practice

Freudian psychology and its derivatives are a complex affair. It has been necessary to introduce the main concepts in some detail because they underscore so much of the work of the psychodynamic practitioner. If she is to make sense of her client and all his actions, she needs to be ever alert to the intricate relationship between past experiences and present behaviours. She will need to understand when anxiety distorts the content of relationships and produces self-defeating behaviour. Within the understanding generated by these theories, diagnosis and treatment can never be brief affairs. They have to grapple with a whole childhood of impaired development.

There are several classic texts that describe psychodynamic casework and its practice in fascinating detail. At this stage I shall make particular use of a book written by Reiner and Kaufman nearly thirty years ago. They offer full and transfixing examples of Freudian casework in full flower. I defy the reader not to recognize at least one of their clients amongst the fifteen cases they discuss.

## Diagnosis

If the ego fails to reconcile the conflicts between the instincts, the real world and the conscience, a degree of mental disturbance, often called a neurosis, will result. In particular, one rather primitive psychic ruse which Freud named 'repression' is a critical cause of the neurotic state. The conflict is literally put out of the conscious mind. This is yet another mechanism of defence, the most primitive in fact:

> But it is essentially an escape, a pretence, a withdrawal from reality and as such is doomed to failure. For what is repressed does not really disappear, but continues to exist in the unconscious portion of the mind. It retains all its instinctual energy, and exerts its influence by sending into consciousness a disguised substitute for itself – a neurotic symptom. Thus the person can find himself behaving in ways which he will admit are irrational, yet which he feels compelled to continue without knowing why. For by repressing something out of his consciousness he has given up effective control over it (Stevenson 1974, p.68).

Freud's developmental approach to the personality locates the origin of repression in early childhood and, as has been described, these repressions are basically sexual in the broad sense. Any upsets in psychosexual developments leave the individual vulnerable to neurotic responses on future occasions of anxiety. As far as many social work clients are concerned, one neurosis in particular is endemic — regression. Regression represents the return to one of the psychic stages at which infantile satisfaction is sought. The client's emotional responses at times of difficulty return to these primitive levels of response. It has been seen how such fixations lead to the oral, anal and phallic adult characters. It is to these client groups that Reiner and Kaufman (1959) turn their attention. They distinguish the bulk of families known to casework agencies. Their treatment requires a special combination of psychoanalytic wisdom and worker maturity, patience and time.

## Treatment

We have considered the way problems are explained, assessed and diagnosed using a psychoanalytic outlook. However, what *aims* follow from this view of the personality and what *methods* might be employed to achieve them? 'The psychoanalyst,' writes Dare (1981):

> Conceives his task as being essentially one of facilitating change in some fundamental relationships that the person has with self and the outside world. Through these changes in personality there will be a discovery of ways of being which do not require recourse to symptom formation and which enhance the capacity to enjoy satisfactory relationships and fulfilment in other life activities. This process is one in which the patient understands much more fully the way he or she works as a person and is aimed at giving the patient the opportunity of being able to change aspects of personality which cause dissatisfaction (p.29).

For Reiner and Kaufman (1959) the goal of casework with clients who have character disorders:

> Should be that of promoting gradual maturation with eventual progression toward more advanced levels of personality development. In other words, the growth process, which was interrupted and distorted by trauma or unfavourable milieu, must be resumed and corrected (p.60).

Nor do you achieve this overnight! In effect, the worker nurtures the client through another dependency relationship, but this time a 'good enough' one in which all the difficulties are 'worked through' successfully.

Whether it is a full-blown analysis for the mildly neurotic or extensive casework treatment for the socially inadequate, the underlying goal, to some degree or other, is the same: to improve self-knowledge. Knowing yourself generally improves rational self-control. You are no longer tossed along by impulses. Such understanding makes for an easier, smoother and happier life. In contrast to the behaviourists who treat outside, external behaviour in order to alter inner states, the psychoanalytically informed worker treats the 'inside' state in order to change behaviour on the outside.

At root, treatment is through talk and conversation, although, in the hands of social workers, actions often speak louder than words as far as clients are concerned. Talking about your thoughts and feelings brings them to the surface, into consciousness and out into the open. They become available for conscious examination. Encouraging people to say whatever comes into their heads, a process known as 'free association', can be more useful than firing a string of questions at them. Letting the patient hear himself say the things he says is part of self-assessment and understanding. However, there are times when the flow of associations stops. The patient 'resists' attempts to explore certain areas. Freud took this as a sign that the analyst was getting close to important matters which were still being repressed. If they could only be brought into consciousness, the patient's ego would be in a better position to gain some control over the id. Once the patient begins to see how his behaviour is being influenced by deeper feelings and ancient experiences, he is on the way to gaining insight into his neuroses and anxieties. The analyst may facilitate this achievement by offering interpretations, linking the occurrence of one piece of behaviour with experiences encountered elsewhere, often in childhood. The patient is helped to understand the workings of his mind. Attention is paid to how one's mental life governs attitudes and relationships. The way a client uses defences may be exactly the sort of thing the social worker wants the client to consider and come to understand.

All of this takes a good deal of time. Patients may be meeting their analysts several times a week for several years. Clients can be visited by their social workers for years on end. Trust in the relationship is of paramount importance. The deep feelings engendered in the client may also colour the relationship. Many of these feelings, particularly the early ones associated with parental relationships in childhood, are transferred to the therapeutic relationship. The worker sees repetitions of experiences that represent problems with relationships which derive ultimately from the client's early life experiences. The client reacts to the worker at such times as if the worker were like his father or mother. This is known as transference. The client transfers past emotions to the present situation. Hence, understanding what is happening in the relationship between the worker and her client is of the utmost importance. Transference may not only distort the therapeutic relationship, but it may also cause the client to confuse other relationships as older feelings are transferred to new, unconnected situations. Health visitors are treated as if they were 'know-all' elder sisters. Lovers become fathers. Transference is said to be taking place when there is a repetition of the past which is inappropriate to the present. To the extent that a person continues to react to the new relationship as if it was an old experience, he is dealing with the real situation inappropriately.

Hutten (1972) describes an example of transference in a piece of social work with the 'O.' family, a skilled working class couple and their three children. The problem was the poor state of the marriage. Mrs O. had had an affair. She was then deserted by her lover. Her husband also threatened to leave her, which precipitated an admission into psychiatric hospital. Except with her lover, she had never achieved sexual satisfaction. Her husband was tentative in all aspects of their relationship which was altogether low-key. The couple were seen by a male psychiatrist and a female social worker. Therapy lasted a year:

> Mr O. was an only child . . . He tended to see his father as exploitative of his mother and aligned himself with her. He was a gentle fellow, wary of getting hurt by women and believing his mother's attitude to sex — that it was something not enjoyed by women. Mrs O. also had a mother who declared that sexual desire was a dirty peculiarity of men's. Her father was a charming seducer who encouraged her to believe that he would take her to live with him when he left her mother. Instead, he took to live with him a teenage girl of his daughter's age (ibid., p.7).

Having established the problem and the couple's background and childhood experiences, the workers made the following diagnosis:

> This marriage was designed to exclude the emergence of a sexually attractive 'seducer' man who might betray Mrs O. as her father and her lover had done, or exploit her as Mr O. had felt his father had exploited his mother (ibid., p.7).

The male worker was seen by the couple as the 'seducer' man. In fact Mrs O. began to find him a source of both fascination and annoyance. In contrast the female worker was seen as exploited by her male partner. Knowledge about unconscious processes enabled the workers to understand what caused the woman to be frigid and her husband tentative: it was 'their shared unconscious antagonism towards sexually attractive, forceful men and their unconscious collusion to keep such a figure out of their marriage'. Moreover, Mrs O.'s need to have an advantage over the men in her life was clearly derived from the disappointment and humiliation she suffered from her father.

Treatment relied heavily on the workers' knowledge and use of transference. The interpretation of the transferences taking place was felt to be most effective in changing unconsciously determined ways of behaving. This is how it was done:

The first sign of an improvement in the O.'s sexual relationship came after two and a half months when their sexual curiosity about the workers during a coming holiday break was interpreted. Their habit of concrete, unsymbolic thinking led them to believe that the workers were in fact having an affair . . . this led Mrs O. to recall that she had repeatedly accompanied her mother to spy on her father making love to other women. When Mr O.'s fears that he had caused his wife's former gynaecological ill-health and their guilt about masturbation had been discussed, the idealisation and hatred of the male psychiatrist/lover diminished. The female worker experienced herself as seen in a very disparaged role and also noticed that it was assumed that she would disapprove of sex. When this was pointed out and related to both their mothers' lack of interest in sex, they were able to return aglow with sexual satisfaction (ibid., p.7).

## The four stages of treatment

Reiner and Kaufman worked with parents of delinquent children. These parents were emotionally fixated at pre-genital levels of development which give rise to disordered personalities. In the face of emotional tensions, such parents employ responses characteristic of the oral, anal and phallic stages of emotional development. Their underlying problem is that of anxiety:

> In treatment, the client's resistance to forming a close relationship with the caseworker must be patiently overcome; he can then be helped to further maturation by techniques designed to help him incorporate ego strength, face his depressive nucleus, and evolve a sense of identity (Reiner and Kaufman 1959, p.18).

At the heart of treatment lies a sound relationship between client and worker. To achieve such a relationship takes time. Trust in relationships has been a bad investment in the past for these clients. They are not going to commit themselves without a lot of testing-out. This could promise a rough time for the worker, especially in the early stages. The social worker has to understand this and not lose heart, and certainly not lose patience. Rejecting the client merely confirms the client's wary and bruised view of what other people offer.

In time trust will develop. The relationship will feel more secure and the client will begin to express feelings of hurt and pain. Gradually the client's ego grows stronger. Short-term therapy can do little for these parents. They need long nurturing, sustaining relationships where trust is found. In effect, the worker is helping them grow up emotionally by offering a sound, realistic and caring relationship. Treatment along these lines is likely to take at least several years. During this time, the parents can resume and correct the emotional development which was interrupted or distorted when they themselves were children. Reiner and Kaufman identify four stages in the treatment process:

1 Establishing a relationship.
2 Ego-building through identification.
3 Helping the client establish a separate identity.
4 Helping the client gain self-understanding.

The first stage of treatment of establishing a relationship is the most difficult. Social workers will find clients displaying a wide and often florid array of 'acting-out' behaviour in the face of the anxieties precipitated by the agency's parental figure image. Techniques of clarification, interpretation and insight are unsuccessful with this group. They simply result in the client's failure to return or cause increases in acting-out:

> In the person with a character disorder, the ghosts of old and fearful relationships are not so easily laid. He needs a long experience of testing out the worker . . . before he is free to participate in therapeutic communication (ibid., p.67).

At the end of this long first stage, the client may well become less guarded, allow himself to care about what the worker thinks, keep appointments and admit that he is sometimes wrong. Such shifts:

> Mean that the client has sufficiently relaxed his fears of closeness, trusting, or dependency to begin cautiously to resume the process of growth and maturation through a relationship with a substitute parental figure (ibid., p.93).

The second stage of ego-building is a gradual one. The client begins to identify with the worker. Eventually the client incorporates many of the worker's ideas and attitudes. He does things as he thinks the worker would do them. The worker can risk more direct attempts to show the parents how to be better mothers or fathers. Encouragement is important. Equally important is the introduction by the worker of a greater sense of reality. Clients are encouraged to view the world more realistically. 'In essence, the caseworker provides a corrective parental experience since the child first learns about reality from adults who care for him' (ibid., p.100).

During the third stage the client is helped to establish a separate identity. This is a difficult time for the client as he launches out into the world on his own. He may regress and return to earlier ways of behaving. He may become angry at the worker:

> Actually this process of separation resembles the process of the adolescent separating from the parent. It involves similar depression, anxiety, hostility, and search for identity . . . No emotional tie is given up without the accompaniment of negative feelings; and in the child's primitive emotional life, dependence is

always identical with love, and the struggle for independence is accompanied by hostility (ibid., pp.122–3).

So what the client needs at this stage is a strong, fair and consistent parental figure who understands the struggle to grow up to become a man or a woman (ibid., p.139).

The fourth and final stage is where the client is helped to understand his behaviour and its roots in the past. This phase can be attempted only if the client has successfully worked through his pre-Oedipal fixations and become emotionally more mature. He can begin to consider his defences, he can ponder the ways in which he responds to frustration and set-back without becoming prey to infantile emotional behaviour. By now his own sense of self is strong. The claim is not that these clients are fully mature, insightful people as a result of casework treatment. Rather, they are no longer stuck with primitive emotions which destroy relationships and are ultimately self-defeating. Their lives are calmer, less crisis-ridden and more controlled. Emotionally they have grown up.

## Conclusion

The typical critic of the social worker and what she does is probably a sociologist who sets up his target to look like a psychoanalytic caseworker, steeped in Freudian psychology, and who talks about potty training experiences with the client while above the roof leaks, at the door the rentman shouts for his money and all around run children without winter coats. It is doubtful whether this worker ever really existed but such an Aunt Sally suits the critic's purpose. She is a myth. Nevertheless the myth persists.

It is true that psychoanalytic thinking has held a fascination for social workers for well over half a century. Yet it must be observed that social workers have never pretended to be peripatetic analysts, serving Freud to the poor in undiluted measure. They have found some bits helpful. The concept of defence mechanisms, the way the past influences the present and the debilitating effects of anxiety have all encouraged social workers to reflect on their clients and their practice in a more thoughtful way. On the whole, social workers have taken what is useful from psychoanalysis and its derivations and adapted it to their own situation.

Some important landmarks have been achieved in social work following this recipe. We might mention the writings of Gordon Hamilton in the 1940s. Certainly, we have to pay our respects to the work of Florence Hollis. In 1964 she brought her thinking together in *Casework: A Psychosocial Therapy*. Note the term psychosocial as well as the word therapy. She was influenced by the ego-psychologists of her day and so felt that social work had to show a greater interest in the relationship between the client and his environment, particularly his social environment. Although social workers had to acknowledge the power of unconscious processes in any situation, it was not their job to deal directly with unconscious material in the psychoanalytical sense. Insight developments and heavy interpretations were not the primary methods of the average caseworker.

Hollis identifies six major treatment procedures, some of which have become part of social work's daily vocabulary. The belief is that clients have to learn to cope with their feelings, their circumstances and the consequences of their behaviour. To help them achieve this, the caseworker provides support and sustainment. She helps them explore and ventilate feelings. Much time is needed to reflect on how the client feels about, affects and is affected by other people as well as difficult situations. Research evidence clearly confirms the prevalence of some of the procedures recognized by Hollis. In practice, support is the most commonly cited aim and activity. In contrast, cure and changing personalities remain relatively rare and specialized pursuits.

Perhaps the conclusions reached by Yelloly (1980) in her definitive study of social work theory and psychoanalysis are the ones, in the end, that we are bound to echo:

> One of the major premises of this book has been that it is essential to draw a clear distinction between the contribution of psychoanalysis to the understanding of human behaviour and emotional life, and its contribution to the methodology of social work. Its impact on the former has in my view been by far the greatest; the treatment techniques of psychoanalysis lie well outside what social work regards as its territorial waters (p.166).

Psychoanalysis has helped social workers to understand personality, behaviour and emotional suffering. It has proved less useful in assisting social workers to develop a set of detailed prescriptions and methods appropriate for use in everyday practice. Even so, let us be in no doubt. The worker who chooses to view her client within a broad Freudian framework displays a highly distinctive style of practice. It can be detected at each stage of the social work process. Poor childhood experiences cause clients to suffer particular emotional problems and personality disorders. These upset the client's emotional, interpersonal and social functioning. The aim, therefore, is to help him or her to mature, to become less emotionally fragile and to function in society. Without question, one of the main vehicles through which these aims have been pursued is that of a trusting, nurturing and long-term relationship between the worker and her client. To understand the dynamics of this relationship is a critical skill.

Periodically there are attempts to tamper with this formula. In particular, there are regular pushes towards shortening the length of the relationship and giving practice a more task-centred focus. This produces a strain between the theory and the practice. Eventually, one or the other has to go in favour of a new partner. Break away movements are common. In developing new practices social workers are obliged to find new theories. Shifts in the direction of 'briefer' casework and task-oriented interventions have seen practitioners drifting further and further away from their original psychodynamic origins towards the camp of the behaviourists. What do we find there? It is to this group that we go next.

# 9 Behavioural Social Work

**Wanted: a prescription for effective practice**

For most social workers, a behavioural approach is either viewed with extreme suspicion or embraced as the answer to a prayer. If wariness is the response, it is rarely because the worker has some intimate working knowledge of behavioural theory and its application. More usually it is because the sceptic holds the popular caricature of behaviourism as something mechanical, manipulative and malign. Yet in spite of its bad press, behavioural social work not only refuses to go away but has positively gained in strength and vigour.

There are several reasons for this, the most important of which is that it is a credible reaction to the regular battering that social work practice has received from research over the last two decades into its effectiveness. Time and time again, researchers and critics alike see social workers lacking a clarity of purpose, possessing a vagueness of method and showing a wishy-washiness that is altogether indefensible. It appears that social workers really will have to mend their sloppy ways if they are ever to earn public support and respect. Enter the behaviourist. Behavioural social work demands of its practitioners that they be purposeful and methodical, organized and scientific, concrete and explicit. Unlike many social work practices, behavioural approaches not only tell the practitioner what is going on (theory) but they go on to advise her exactly what to do in a clearly prescribed fashion (method). Being told what to do and how to do it come as something of a godsend to many social workers.

In general, behavioural social workers like to tackle behaviours that are observable, measurable and amenable to description in concrete terms. So, rather than talk about seven-year-old Danny being an aggressive little boy, the behavioural worker would want to learn, amongst other things, that he punches particular classmates every time they tease him which happens at playtimes and during loosely structured lessons and that, if the teacher attempts to break up the ensuing fight, she too will be hit by Danny. Problems are defined into small, identifiable pieces of behaviour. They are dealt with discretely. Goals are set and mutually agreed with clients. Involvement proceeds by way of small, sequential, manageable steps.

Three very important attitudes characterize practice in this field: it is problem-focused, task-centred and time-limited. In this, of course, behavioural social work is similar to the other techniques that arose in response to social work's alleged woolliness. The problem-solving approach of Perlman (1957), the task-centred methods developed by Reid and Epstein (1972) and crisis intervention techniques have many features in common with behavioural social work. In general, the effect of all these approaches has been to sharpen the way in which social workers organize and structure their practice.

Behavioural social work sees itself as a science applying:

> The principles of learning and social learning theories to the analysis and modification of behaviour. These principles are derived from empirical research into how behaviour is learned, maintained and unlearned (Hudson and Macdonald 1986, p.2).

In essence, although the theories held and the techniques employed are relatively simple, practice itself can be highly intricate and refined. The good practitioner applies behavioural principles with skill, care and considerable imagination. Great patience is called for in order to appreciate all the actions and reactions that surround a given piece of behaviour. Dogged and insistent questioning is necessary if a detailed understanding is to be gained of exactly what happens before, during and after a problematic event. The social worker has to build up a picture of all the factors which may have a bearing on the behaviour under investigation.

So, when Jane, a difficult, tempestuous adolescent, storms out of the house not to return until the early hours of the morning, we need to discover that prior to her departure she had a row with her mother. We need to know that the sequence of events in which mother and daughter antagonize each other follows the same old pattern. Mother makes an issue over pocket money and her daughter being surly and ungrateful. Jane accuses her mother of nagging and prying into her affairs. Eventually when Jane does return, her mother refuses to speak, but her father frets and fusses until his daughter is safely in bed.

It will be necessary to return to this style of inquiry in a while, but first we need to outline the theories that underpin these behavioural performances. In particular we shall consider respondent conditioning, operant conditioning and social learning theory (also known as modelling). Most writers in this field discuss cognitive theory as it influences the techniques of behaviour modification. The theoretical stage having been set, we shall then be in a strong position to introduce the 'behavioural intervention procedures'.

## Respondent conditioning

When a stimulus that previously did not evoke a particular response then does so, that response is said to be conditional on the appearance of that stimulus.

If the previous sentence does not sound immediately familiar then the mention of Ivan Pavlov and his dogs probably will for it was the Russian physiologist who pioneered work in this area. His drooling dogs are now part of behavioural folklore. Dogs salivate naturally (unconditionally) at the sight of food. If a tuning fork is sounded (for it was a tuning fork and not a bell, we are reminded by Hudson and Macdonald 1986, pp.22−3) just before the presentation of the food, it is only a matter of time before the dog salivates at the sound of the tuning fork alone. Vibrating forks now stimulate salivation as a conditioned response.

Similarly, human beings automatically start with fear at a sudden loud noise. Babies may even cry. If you are feeling rather unfriendly towards babies, it would be possible to condition them to howl at the sight of an object that previously evoked no concern whatsoever. This was the fate of Little Albert. This baby showed no innate fear of a tame white rat introduced into his play pen. He even played with it. Then Watson and Raynor (1920) began their experiment. Each time the rat was introduced to Albert, a metal bar was struck emitting a loud, penetrating clang. This made the baby cry. In no time at all, Little Albert learned to fear the rat, even without the accompanying sound of the metal bar.

Moreover, the stimulus that evokes the response can become 'generalized'. This means that things that sound like tuning forks, such as bells or xylophones, may also cause dogs to salivate. Although furry white rats may be the initial conditioned stimulus for young babies, the fear may generalize so that the appearance of other furry animals such as rabbits or cats or even the wearing of a fur coat may also play havoc with the infant's peace of mind.

The combination of respondent conditioning and its generalization has a powerful impact on the lives of many people as they go about their daily lives. A bad experience with a nasty dog may cause the hapless victim untold difficulties as he worries about how to plot his route to work avoiding all the places where dogs may lurk. Being physically abused by your stepfather may generate not only a fear of him but may generalize to a fear and avoidance of all men. This could well create problems when the child goes to school and is taught by male teachers or when she falls ill and is seen by a doctor who is a man. A good many 'phobias', anxiety-states and other severely debilitating physical and emotional responses can be understood in terms of learning through respondent conditioning.

The important fact to note throughout these examples is that something happens *and then* the response occurs. The stimulus triggers the reaction. A hamster appears and the baby cries, a trip to the shops and the agoraphobic experiences blind panic. It is this order of events which gives a clue to the nature of the respondent treatment procedures. They not only explain how these debilitating behaviours were learned in the first place, but they also suggest ways in which they can be unlearned.

Some fears, of course, are reasonable and realistic. If a father is brutal to his daughter or a woman fears walking in a neighbourhood known for its sexual violence, then there is little point in attempting to help them feel more comfortable in what after all is a dangerous situation. Hudson and Macdonald (1986) provide many examples of behavioural social work. They introduce their section on respondent procedures by stating that the key principle is to break the connection between the stimulus and the unwanted response whilst, at the same time, introducing a new, desirable response. Relaxation training has proved most beneficial in this field. The ability to relax in situations that once produced only tension and anxiety is invaluable. Perhaps the most widespread technique used is that of systematic desensitization. It is used most often in treating people who are extremely anxious or fearful in what, to others, appear to be reasonable circumstances. This is how it works.

Systematic desensitization involves introducing something pleasant at the same time that the anxiety-provoking stimulus occurs. The principle is exactly the same as that which occurs with Pavlov's dogs and Little Albert, except now the intent is to produce not a conditioned fear but a conditioned pleasure. The strength of the pleasure must outweigh the strength of the anxiety. Pleasurable feelings can be brought about through being relaxed and calm, enjoying reassuring company or simply sucking a sweet. The client chooses. Usually several stages are involved:

1   After the worker and client determine precisely what it is that arouses the anxiety, the worker helps the client establish a hierarchy of situations ranging from those with which it is easy to cope right through to those which produce the greatest panic and fear. For example, the agoraphobic may feel reasonably at ease collecting milk from the door step, less comfortable walking out into the street and absolutely terrified at the prospect of shopping in the city. It may take a while to help a client identify each level in this hierarchy which may have as many as ten steps.

2   In some techniques, the client is asked to imagine each step, starting at the lowest. At the same time they are asked to relax completely in the ways taught. Eventually the pleasure that the relaxation induces outweighs the moderate fear of the first step so that the first anxiety level disappears altogether, evoking no unpleasant feelings. This is repeated for each successive step until one-by-one they are reduced to a zero-level of anxiety.

3   However, good practice encourages the client to experience the situation for real — *in vivo*. In the case of the agoraphobic, as well as relaxing, the supporting presence of the worker or a friend may

act as the initial pleasant stimulus. The increasing feeling of confidence in a situation that previously caused fear acts as a further stimulus. Such procedures are strongly recommended because they return the client to the actual upsetting situation and desensitize him or her directly to it. Hudson and Macdonald (1986, p.122) give the example of a school phobic (always assuming that there is not a real playground bully of whom the child is quite rightly frightened). Each step is introduced and counterposed with the pleasant stimulus. When the client experiences no anxiety he moves on to the next step, thus:

(i)     Walking past school (with social worker, then alone).
(ii)    Standing outside school at weekend (with social worker, then alone).
(iii)   In school with social worker at weekend.
(iv)    In classroom with teacher at weekends.
(v)     In playground with social worker on schoolday.
(vi)    In school building on schoolday but not in class.
(vii)   In school, in class with other children.

Respondent conditioning procedures are used widely to treat various phobias and anxiety states met all too commonly in social work. For many social work clients, these anxiety-states are not mild afflictions. They ruin lives. They permeate every fabric of the family's functioning. Agoraphobic mothers may never venture out of the house. Depression sets in. Eldest daughters are kept off school to do the shopping and collect the younger children from nursery. Help is needed desperately and systematic desensitization, as a well-tried and tested procedure, is something of a success story in these cases.

### Operant conditioning (or instrumental conditioning)

Here, rather than something or someone in the environment eliciting a response from the individual as in respondent conditioning, the individual brings about a response to which the environment reacts. The individual's behaviour is instrumental in producing an environmental event. The individual behaves and then something happens. The individual actively and often purposefully operates on the environment, particularly when that environment is other people; the environment reacts in such a way as to influence the subsequent occurrence of the original action or behaviour. Again, some examples will help.

A toddler screams and a bag of crisps appears. The husband sulks and the wife comforts and indulges him. The teenager cleans her room and receives smiles, praise and pocket money. In these cases it is likely that rewarding screams with crisps, sulks with cuddles and housework with money will reinforce, and so increase the future likely perform-ance of the behaviour in question.

In contrast, some behaviours are punished. Punishers are environmental reactions which have the effect of decreasing the future
occurrence of a piece of behaviour. If a mother's efforts to show a
friendly interest in her daughter's schooling are rebuffed, it will not
be long before the girl is greeted with hurt silence upon her return
home from school and the friendly interest disappears.

Operant behaviours abound in social work. When the normal give
and take of everyday life goes astray we witness the full meanness and
self-defeating repertoire of human behaviour at its most sad and point-
less. Marriages fall apart from lack of mutual rewards, children learn
all the wrong behaviours and mentally handicapped adults struggle
without a few, simple, basic social skills. If the social worker can learn
to intervene in these behavioural roundabouts, there is the prospect
of new interactional styles being learned. However, before considering
how she might set about doing this, it is necessary to look at one more
way in which a behaviour can be weakened to the point of extinction.

If a reinforcer is removed, the incentive to perform that behaviour
gradually diminishes to the point of extinction. If a child who throws
a temper tantrum normally gets his mother running to him full of
concern and attention, it may soon reach the stage when she cannot
leave him alone in a room for more than a few seconds or let someone
else take over his care without his screaming and yelling. Attention
nearly always acts as a reinforcer, no matter whether it's love or anger.
Difficult as it will be at first, the mother will be advised to ignore
completely, and without exception, each one of her son's outbursts.
Without the reward the temper tantrums will, in time, cease. When he
is playing quietly and acceptably, the mother is advised to join the
boy, giving him love and attention. This combined strategy rewards
and therefore promotes the desired behaviour whilst extinguishing the
bad. The effect of combining reinforcement and extinction procedures
is generally the preferred method of intervention. Punishment
procedures have unfortunate 'side-effects' and are not recommended
except in extreme circumstances (see Sheldon 1982, pp.69–70 for a
discussion on this matter).

The following example is given by Vevers who, as a local authority
social worker, describes a piece of behavioural social work. The involvement was modest but effective. It illustrates nicely how reinforcement
and extinction procedures might be combined in everyday practice.

Anthony, reports Vevers (1981), was a two-and-three-quarter-year-
old boy whose extremely demanding behaviour had led the social
worker to encourage his mother to place him in a local day nursery.
One Friday morning, Jan and Karen, the nursery workers responsible
for Anthony, telephoned Paul Vevers to announce that the boy was
unmanageable. Anthony had frequent temper tantrums and was
consistently defiant. Something had to be done.

What, in fact, the social worker did was to adopt a behavioural approach designed to tackle the problem head on. However, the first thing to be done was to establish exactly what was the problem in terms of concrete actions. 'So we defined the problem in terms of Anthony's visible behaviour. "Being violent" meant hitting, kicking, or biting and "being disruptive" meant refusing to obey a specific instruction from Karen or Jan.'

The next task was to isolate one of these behaviours and focus on its treatment. Anthony's defiance was particularly troublesome for the nursery staff. They were highly motivated to rid him of this attitude and so this was selected as the target behaviour. Rather than approach it negatively, the decision was to make the intervention more positive, preferring to increase his desirable behaviours rather than seeking only to eliminate the undesirable ones. 'So we rephrased our aim as being to encourage Anthony to do what Jan and Karen said more often.'

The treatment also included taking steps to avoid creating a situation in which it was known that Anthony would have a tantrum. In the trade these are known as 'antecedent controls':

> For example, Anthony had a (variable) favourite colour and would often get very upset if given the wrong colour plate or mug. It was often possible for the nursery staff to avoid a show-down by checking in advance which colour he wanted that day. As the nursery matron was later to remark, the willingness of the staff to avoid unnecessary battles of will prevented many incidents of defiance every arising (ibid.).

Even so, this still left an unacceptable number of instances of defiance during the rest of the day. How frequent and intense were these disruptions? The social worker decided to do two things: make a baseline, and then compare Anthony's behaviour with children whose behaviour was acceptable:

> I went to the nursery on three occasions, for one hour, and recorded every instruction given to Anthony by Jan and Karen, whether he complied or not, and every tantrum which involved hitting, kicking or biting.

Two other children were also observed along similar measures. Success was defined as when Anthony's compliance reached the same frequency as the 'control' children.

By a process of painstaking observation the hunch that adult attention, of whatever kind, simply acted as a reward for the boy's misbehaviour was confirmed. Attention simply maintained his disruptiveness:

> One well-tried solution is to use 'time out'. This meant, basically, removing Anthony from all attention when he was disruptive.

That is when he did not comply with a specific request. This would involve putting him outside the room or in a corner of the garden. Time out was to end once Anthony had been quiet for a brief period . . . Jan and Karen now had to give instructions to Anthony in a clear and loud voice. If Anthony did not comply, the instruction was repeated with the warning that he would 'go outside' if he did not obey. On the occasions when he still did not comply, Jan or Karen took him, wordlessly (so as not to give him attention) and placed him in the preselected time-out place. However, more important than this was that Jan and Karen made a fuss of Anthony when he did obey (thus rewarding his good behaviour) (ibid., p.13).

As usually happens in extinction procedures, the target behaviour gets worse before it gets better. The workers were prepared for this. Patience and perseverence are vital at this stage. Eventually things began to improve. The social worker observed and measured Anthony's behaviour after the intervention. There was considerable improvement. Before treatment, in a typical hour he would have four temper tantrums and receive up to fifty-nine orders from Karen or Jan of which he complied only with 26 per cent. In a similar hour, the 'non-problem' children showed no tantrums, each receiving an average of thirteen orders with which 68 per cent were complied. After the behavioural programme, Anthony managed an hour without losing his temper. Fourteen orders were issued and he complied with 57 per cent of them. Even after the formal intervention programme was completed, the improvement continued. In conclusion, one of the nursery staff described the new and improved Anthony thus: 'when we used to split the children up into groups, nobody wanted to take Anthony with them. Well, everybody seems to enjoy having him in their group now'.

## Social learning or modelling

A great deal of what we learn is achieved by watching other people do things. Children learn many behaviours, both good and bad, from their parents through modelling. Imitation and practice of a desired behaviour usually leads to its successful performance:

Whilst the respondent and operant paradigm seem, on some interpretations, to adequately account for the continued occurrence of behaviours, it is modelling that appears best fitted to account for the way in which most behaviour is learned in the first instance. Modelling accounts for the acquisition of a vast range of very different behaviours: skills simple and complex, from washing dishes to brain surgery, from social good manners to conducting philosophical debate (Hudson and Macdonald 1986, p.41).

In his development of this model of learning, Bandura (1977, p.59) also notes that the individual's own view of things plays an important part. He or she will have ideas about the behaviour observed that suit their interests. How easy is it? How useful will it be? What benefits might be expected? The observer notes the consequences when a piece of behaviour is performed and so may choose to learn it.

Modelling works best when the model is liked, respected and seen to be successful. Several steps are present in a formal modelling programme (ibid., p.141; Sheldon 1982, p.182):

1  Identify the behaviour to be learned.
2  Arrange a demonstration.
3  Ask the observer to imitate the behaviour.
4  Provide feedback and reinforcement.
5  Repeat demonstration, if necessary.
6  Allow observer to practise until the behaviour is learned.

Social workers use modelling to help clients handle difficult or worrisome encounters such as a visit to the rent tribunal, playing with a fretful child or an appearance in court. Social skills training, so popular with social workers, uses many of the principles of social learning and the techniques of modelling. 'Watch me' and 'practice makes perfect', although not guarantors of success, are likely to improve the performance of clients who, in the past, have produced behaviours that, at best, can only be described as inept.

### Behavioural programmes for intervention
Behavioural social work has proved attractive to social workers because it demands two interesting things of their practice. Firstly the worker has to make explicit her practice assumptions; and, secondly, these assumptions have to be shared with the client. A good example of how to start a behavioural practice with children and their parents is found in Herbert, *Behavioural Treatment of Problem Children: A Practice Manual* (1981). Indeed, in Appendix IV, Herbert provides the reader with a copy of the printed handout which he gives to parents. This explains the theoretical and practical basis on which his treatment programme works in language which is accessible and intelligible to any lay person. Here is an extract:

> The basic idea which you need to know is that your child will tend to repeat any behaviours which bring him some beneficial outcome or 'pay-off' and tend to avoid those behaviours that fail to produce rewards. In other words, your child will only continue to perform those behaviours which are worthwhile and rewarding to him, and he will stop performing behaviours which do not give him any rewards.

You have used this idea to teach your child many things without knowing it. Some of the things you have taught him will be the things you do want him to do, but unfortunately it is also easy to teach a child to do things you do not want him to do. Of course you teach your child to do socially desirable things in many different ways: you set an example, you instruct, praise and encourage. All these methods are used in behaviour therapy in order to provide the youngster with alternative (and happier) ways of solving his problems and difficulties. This is but one way of looking at treatment. It may be the parents, as much as the child, who need some assistance in re-thinking their management of the child. There is no more reason to be embarrassed about this than going to the doctor for advice about his health and physical well-being (ibid., p.211).

Such an open declaration of what you understand and how you intend to proceed is still unusual in social work practice. Behaviourists are very clear on the order and content of their practice procedure. You may have noticed already the tendency in this chapter to enumerate practice steps in a crisp one, two, three fashion. I am simply reflecting the way behaviourists do it. In fact, all the basic introductory behavioural textbooks prescribe a similar intervention sequence. It goes something like this:

1   Identify the client's complaint or problem.
2   Establish what he or she wants to change.
3   Analyze the conditions that control the problem behaviour and determine which behaviours can be changed.
4   Select and state goals.
5   Plan and execute a treatment programme to achieve these goals.

Behavioural work uses a basic learning equation called the ABC analysis. In every instance, the worker needs to establish, in detail, what happens before, during and after the occurrence of the problem behaviour. The practitioner, therefore, needs to pay great attention to:

Antecedent   →   The Behaviour   →   Consequences
events             in question

The problem behaviour has to be described in terms that are observable and measurable. Its frequency, intensity and duration have to be found. It is no good a wife describing her husband as moody. She needs to say that after she returns from her car maintenance class he does not speak for the next two hours, he stares with determined concentration at the television and provocatively makes himself a cup of cocoa without offering to make her one at the same time.

Problem behaviours can be described as either excessive (too much of an undesirable behaviour such as shouting, fighting or stealing) or deficient (not enough of a desired behaviour such as talking, eating or going to school). As will be seen, the general aim is to decrease excessive behaviours and increase deficient ones. Such a detailed description of the problem gives the worker a 'baseline' from which to measure the future performance of both the problem behaviour and the preferred behaviour, particularly after treatment. How else do you know if your efforts have been effective?

The next step is to analyze thoroughly the circumstances surrounding the problem behaviour. We need to know what triggers a behaviour and what supports it. We need to know what behaviours are absent which those concerned would like to see present. Behavioural social workers prefer to ask *what* questions and not *why* questions. 'Hence,' suggest Ullman and Krasner (1969):

> The worker might ask: What is the person doing? Under what conditions are particular behaviours being performed? What are the effects of those behaviours, that is, what changes occur after they are emitted? What situations are being avoided? What environmental circumstances are maintaining the behaviour? What environmental circumstances can be altered to diminish maladaptive behaviour and increase adaptive behaviour? What reinforcers can be supplied (by the social worker or significant others)? Most important, the social worker asks, what does the client want?

As you will gather, this detailed exploration of the problem allows both worker and client to build up a thorough appreciation of how difficulties arise, remain and persist. This measured appreciation in itself goes a long way towards understanding and altering old habits.

At all times during this investigative stage the worker needs to be ascertaining who does what, where, when, with whom and with what effect (Sheldon 1982, p.99). If all these questions are answered we have a behavioural assessment. This will provide strong hints about what elements in the situation can be changed and modified. It will offer clues about what alternative responses are available.

Mark's mother rants and raves every time he steals from her purse. He is eight and the problem is getting worse. We also discover that she appears to give all her time and attention to the baby that arrived belatedly and unexpectedly in the household six months earlier. After one of the stealing episodes and mum's frantic response, dad, who normally says little, takes his son quietly aside once the furore has died down and attempts to understand the boy's apparently puzzling and exasperating behaviour. He has even been known to slip Mark a couple of pounds 'if it's money you want son'. We learn that Mark wants attention and affection from his mother, but appears only to receive a warped, ill-tempered version (which is better than nothing) when he steals from her. He does not take money from anybody else. We understand that Mark's father comes into action, offering a sigh and confused sympathy, only when there is trouble. Other times he just sits, puffs his pipe and watches the television. By modifying the environment (in this case mum and dad's behaviour), the social worker and the family can re-shape the pattern of responses, say through a combination of extinction and reinforcement procedures, so that the stealing stops and well-timed attentions return.

Of course, there has to be agreement by all concerned. The worker not only spends a great deal of time making a behavioural assessment, she needs the people involved to recognize what she is saying and agree that this is the way things happen. They need also to agree what behaviours are to be changed and how this should take place. Goals are formulated in terms of increasing, decreasing and maintaining particular target behaviours. In practice these are translated into specific, concrete and observable responses to be produced in set situations by identified individuals. These objectives, according to Herbert (1981, p.75), must determine the following four elements:

1   Who will do?
2   What?
3   To what extent?
4   Under what conditions?

Contracts, sometimes verbal and often written, record who has agreed to do what and when. They may contain such things as 'We the parents agree not to criticize Samantha's clothes or choice of friends' while Samantha for her part agrees 'to let her mother know where she is going after school if it is not directly home'.

## A science for a disciplined practice

When all the assessing has been explored, the objectives clarified and contracts agreed, the behavioural programme is allowed to run. The worker has established a baseline from which to judge progress. At the end of the programme run, the worker and her clients can sit down and review the outcome. We are in solid 'functionalist' territory here. Behavioural social workers are proud to claim that their roots lie firmly in the soils of science. Behaviour can be viewed objectively. It can be caused, it can be measured. A behaviour is a *problem* when it is 'maladaptive', creating upsets in family functioning, school attendance and social conformity.

If the external environment is the most important cause of behaviour, then the most important environment is that of other people and the way they act and respond. Mothers and children, husbands and lovers, teachers and peers all have a powerful effect on the way we behave. We all try to affect, indeed control, the behaviour of other people by the things we say and do. In turn we are affected by the way they behave towards us. We attempt to influence others by reasoning or through instruction; we try to control them through anger or smiles. Understanding the part that reinforcements, punishments and models play in shaping our behaviour allows us to *explain* what people are doing to each other. All such behaviours are observable. They are there for anyone to see and record.

It soon becomes clear what the participants in a behavioural programme want to change. The preferred behavioural condition of the participants becomes the goal. Goals have to be stated in observable terms.

Unlike many social work theories, behavioural knowledge is capable of direct application in human affairs. It offers precise methods of practice. Behavioural social work not only tells the worker how to understand what is going on, it prescribes in step-by-step detail how to do something about it if that is the wish of the participants. If people can shape other people's behaviour through the pattern of their responses, we can use this fact to therapeutic advantage. If you are utterly indifferent to the struggles I have expressing my feelings then I shall soon become silent in your company. Show me some interest and a sympathetic ear and I may well reveal my most burning emotions. By modifying and fixing interpersonal stimuli and responses, we can eliminate undesirable behaviours. Teaching people to respond differently has a powerful effect on a situation's behavioural content. The shy can learn to be bold, the urges of the impulsive can be kept in check and the vicious circles of bloody-mindedness can give way to benign spirals of mutual reward.

The sequence 'problem-assessment-goal-methods' is to be recognized in all books taking a behavioural approach to social work. Behavioural theories and their application seem to impose a common style both on the content and writing of such books, particularly the large number that emanate from America. They really do read more like car maintenance manuals than experiential mysteries or Freudian who-done-its or political thrillers. They are eminently practical, though inclined to be dull. Most behavioural texts are packed with examples. They offer the social worker who feels she needs to get to a grip on welfare work's slippery surfaces a good, strong foothold, so long as she does not ask too many questions of an epistemological nature.

Herbert (1981) provides the child care worker with the quintessential practice manual. The practitioner is guided skilfully and logically through every stage of practice. In parts she is almost given a script of what to say and when to say it, so detailed is the exposition. However, for a livelier style we might turn to another book, mentioned several times previously, by Hudson and Macdonald (1986). Theirs is a more general introduction and, unlike Herbert, they speak directly to social workers. They offer dozens of illustrations that are immediately relevant to social work, and yet, like all behavioural texts, they demand of the practitioner the same systematic sequence of thought and action. The result is a disciplined practice that tempts those workers who are desperate to cut a swathe of clear thinking through the tangle of everyday social work.

As a group, behaviourists have introduced social workers to a style of practice which is in marked contrast to the psychodynamic tradition. There is an emphasis on the present rather than the past. There is a preference for taking note of the external and observable and not the internal and reported. Yet both approaches share a view that the failings lie in the individual and that it is to the individual that treatments are addressed. Thinking for both Freudians and behaviourists is causal and scientific. It is the individual and his pathological state that has to be treated and cured before that person can be pronounced socially fit. It is on this basis that we can consider both approaches within the same paradigm, with the prize going to the behaviourists for the most unequivocal support for science and its application.

# 10  The Seekers After Meaning

## Interpretivism

The social world, according to the humanistically inclined, can only be understood subjectively. We have to know how things look from the point of view of those involved. Their ideas and intentions have to be appreciated. The emphasis on the subjective experiences of people discourages interest in society's larger structural characteristics. Nevertheless, implicit in the paradigm is that social affairs are conducted in a regular and ordered manner. Human exchanges occur within the settled rhythms of a stable society.

Theorists of this persuasion, therefore, assume a sociology of regulation. Little is said about society as a whole. The key task, then, is to interpret the individual's actions and utterances in an attempt to gauge how the world appears to the subject. This being the hallmark of this group of theorists, we need to say some more on the matter of subjectivity.

The human spirit is free. People act intentionally, they do not merely behave. They have a sense of purpose. No biology nor any social environment necessarily determines what they do. The net effect of all these individual actions is to create social situations. Out of social interaction emerges the social world.

People impose their own order and meaning on events. It is one of the remarkable abilities of the human mind that it can structure its own experiences. Situations and circumstances mean something. People do have ideas about what is going on. They do not respond passively to impersonal forces. The ideas people have about what is going on themselves become part of the very social situation in which they are found. This is why it is so important to try to understand how the social world looks from the viewpoint of those who comprise it. It is no good emulating the natural sciences. There are no immutable laws of human behaviour. People actively create their world and themselves in it. Studying people objectively tells us nothing of their hopes, plans or feelings. We have to find ways of seeing things from their point of view. Human meaning is taken to be the basic 'stuff' of social science.

The result of this fundamental assumption about the nature of social reality is a distinctive definition of what knowledge is like for the behavioural and social theorist. If reality is socially constructed, it is the job of the social scientist to understand subjective experience.

The subjective meaning of social action has to be interpreted by those who wish to make sense of people and their society. Talking about a particular brand of interpretivism, Burrell and Morgan (1979) note:

> The way in which social reality reflects a precarious balance of intersubjectively shared meanings, which are continually negotiated, sustained and changed through the everyday interaction of individual human beings. Social reality is for them either reaffirmed or created afresh in every social encounter (p.253).

It has been hinted already that a reality that is socially constructed requires a very different set of methods for its examination to those found in the natural sciences. People cannot be studied as if they were objects, just like any other materials in the environment. The social investigator has to understand subjective meanings. It is vital to capture the experience of the other.

Alfred Schutz (1899–1959) developed many of the ground rules for interpretative sociology. He believed the central task of social science was to understand the social world from the point of view of those living within it, using constructs and explanations that are intelligible in terms of the commonsense interpretations of everyday life. Above all else, theorists within this paradigm want to make sense of how people understand their day-to-day experiences and how this affects the way they act and feel towards other people.

They do this using a variety of methods. Some adopt the lifestyle of those under study, hoping to experience their world first hand. Others may ask people how things look to them, what was it they were trying to achieve, how matters turned out. Close observations of what people actually do and say in particular situations helps explain how social realities are built up and how they evolve. But whatever the method, the overriding aim is to capture subjective meanings. If the meaning is lost, you are left with a series of colourless observations which tell you nothing of social interest. It would be like describing the work of Cézanne in terms of the drying characteristics of oil paints or the frequency distribution of the colours used. The result, in terms of art and creativity, is meaningless.

The impact of this approach and its search for social reality has rumbled deep below the surface of the social and behavioural sciences. It offers an argument for quality and not quantity, for experience and not measurement. It has clear implications for social workers and their practice. The level at which the client is viewed depends largely on what the social worker wants to know, understand and do. Two broad interpretative strands have weaved their way into social work. The first includes the client-centred approaches which are derived from humanist psychologies. The second considers the work of the 'interactionists' whose inspiration has come from the influence which phenomenology has had on sociology.

## The client-centred approaches

Respecting the client, valuing his view of events, allowing him to explore his own meanings, all these have proved a very popular sentiment with social workers. Most exponents of the practice believe themselves to be 'non-directive'. That is, they believe they follow the client's own view of his problems and needs. Helping him explore his own feelings, perceptions and meanings is, in itself, therapeutic and beneficial.

Psychologists such as Carl Rogers and George Kelly regard the individual as best placed to understand himself or herself, not some external expert. This is in sharp contrast to the Freudians and behaviourists of whom Bannister (1966) offers the following caricature:

> Psychoanalytic theories seem to suggest that man is basically a battle-field. He is a dark cellar in which a well-bred spinster lady and a sex-crazed monkey are forever engaged in mortal combat, the struggle being refereed by a rather nervous bank clerk. Alternatively, learning theory seems to suggest that man is basically a ping-pong ball with a memory (p.21).

Rogers and Kelly are concerned with the whole person. For them, people are not driven by inner urges or controlled by their environment but are at all times actively trying to make sense of their experience (Peck and Whitlow 1975, p.38).

The social worker attempts to understand and share the client's situation. By establishing a climate of trust and warmth, the client feels confident enough to face up to his own actions. He recovers responsibility for his feelings and behaviour. Once more he can take charge of his own future and destiny. As Whittaker (1974, p.100) sees it, 'the goal of therapy is the client's achievement of a firm sense of wholeness and a fuller experiencing of freedom and autonomy'.

Although the client-centred approach was developed in psychotherapy particularly under the influence of Rogers, it does excite social workers. The relationship between client and worker is taken to be all-important. It must possess qualities of genuineness, empathy and warmth. We are capable of free choices and with the help and interest of another, we can forge our own lives, free of the anxieties that holds us down and back.

Initially fashioned in individual counselling, the client-centred approach has since been applied to work with families and small groups. It is attractive to social workers because it tells them how to 'be' when they 'relate' to clients. It appeals to the humanistic outlook of the 'helping' professions. Above all, not only does it prompt a working style for the practitioner, qualitatively it informs the rest of her social life. It is more a philosophy than a straightforward applied theory. 'Experiential' methods of relating, learning and working are pursued. Subjective meanings and the importance of feelings are valued. Good, open working relationships, with clients and colleagues alike, require that subjective states are recognized and shared. We should care about the other's experience and the other should feel comfortable with them, with us.

In the words of Halmos, it all adds up to a 'ministration of love', the sentiments of which are summed up nicely by Butrym (1976):

> The main tenets underlying these arguments are the primacy of love over science and technology, and hence the effectiveness of 'relationship therapy' over and above all other forms of human intervention in human problems; tenets which are in turn derived from a view of human nature as constantly in the making and capable of growth and improvement, as opposed to a more deterministic orientation (p.27).

I have mentioned Carl Rogers already. His influence, however, has been so pervasive throughout all the helping professions, and in particular social work, that he bears closer scrutiny.

Freud saw people essentially as biologically determined organisms. His view of human nature was pessimistic. In the main, its brutish qualities had to be kept in check. America, however, is alien soil to this gloomy psychology. Rogers simplified matters greatly, adding generous measures of optimism and hope to the human condition. For him, the primary human drive is towards self-actualization. People have the positive potential to become more fully human.

Therapy, help, counselling or what you will comes down to talking. People, everywhere, are looking for other people to hear their troubles. And behind the listening ear are love and genuineness, empathy and warmth. There is nothing intellectually or technically complicated about helping another. It really is no more than just good old human kindness, if given a chance, that always wins the day. Of course, in order for this to happen, we have to be in touch with our emotions, our experience, our intuitive selves. We should trust our 'gut feelings' and not be afraid to express them. Experience is a most important guide to what is real. Throughout the writings of this school, there is a vigorous anti-intellectualism which social workers pick up with glee.

As he grew disillusioned with psychoanalysis, Rogers developed a practice which reverses most Freudian-based techniques. The therapist is not a technical expert. The client actually knows best what is wrong, what needs to be explored and what has to be done. The relationship between client and worker is of critical importance. In fact, believes Clare (1981, p.37), the therapy is less a set of techniques and more a system of values, a philosophy for living. The therapist has to listen sensitively in order to get inside the world of the other. This is helped enormously by the worker learning to respond to experience, as it happens, and not lose it through a lens of cloudy intellectualism which merely increases the distance between the worker and what is really going on. This is how Luborsky and his colleagues describe what Rogerian therapy means to the client:

> An exploration of increasingly strange and unknown and dangerous feelings in himself, the exploration proving possible only because he is gradually realising that he is accepted unconditionally. Thus he becomes acquainted with elements of his experience which in the past have been denied to awareness as too threatening, too damaging to the structures of the self . . . And as he lives these widely varied feelings . . . he discovers that he has experienced himself, that he is all these feelings. He finds his behaviour changing in constructive fashion in accordance with his newly experienced self. He approaches the realisation that he no longer needs to fear what experience may hold, but can welcome it freely as a part of his changing and developing self (quoted in Clare 1981, p.41).

Clare, himself a psychiatrist, toured California and met Rogers. Clare puts the ubiquitous appeal of the client-centred therapies down to their simple and cosy, even sentimental and naïve view of human nature and the human condition. He feels that they take all the hard work out of living and the struggle to cope. It seemed inevitable that America in general and California in particular should be the breeding ground of the first personal growth psychologies.

## Interactionist social work

The brew here is less heady. The talk is not so much of the 'relationship' but rather of 'interaction'; less the feeling of love and more the methodological need for empathy. However, the basic ingredients of the paradigm are fully present. People are seen to be acting purposefully. Their actions take account of what others say and do. Interpretations are made of what is happening. Meanings are imposed. It is within the interactions that occur between people that situations become defined and social reality takes on its meaning. People act purposefully, but they act on the basis of what they believe to be the case.

Perhaps the most exciting concept to emerge from this theoretical school, at least as far as social workers are concerned, is that of labelling. The process by which certain kinds of action become labelled as deviant or abnormal holds great fascination. Of critical importance is the 'audience reaction' to an initially 'deviant act' (Roche 1973, p.223). It is emphasized that a person's action is deviant only because other people choose to define it as such. Whittington and Holland (1985) offer a crisp digest of the main features of the theory. They say that:

> The notion of a socially constructed self-identity is . . . significant in the interactionist approach to mental illness, mental handicap, crime, the use of hard drugs, child abuse and other social problems which are expressed collectively, of course, as 'deviance'. The approach concentrates on the process by which people are labelled as deviant, their reactions to the label, and the reactions of the labeller and others. In this analysis, 'social groups create deviance by making the rules whose infraction constitute deviance' . . . Once labelled, they will find others organising responses to them in terms of the label and be expected to respond accordingly. Gradually, a complex social process produces a redefinition of self, a reorganisation of behaviour in accordance with the deviant identity (p.39).

The analysis has challenging implications for each stage of a social worker's practice. Clients are not 'measured' by any behavioural or psychological yardstick. Instead, their experiences have to be understood, the subjective meaning of their actions appreciated. The social worker, therefore, is primarily interested in getting inside the world of the client and looking out, and not remaining on the outside and simply looking in. Meanings are generated within particular social contexts, such as a marriage, the family, the school and the legal process. We also learn to recognize and understand ourselves in these intimate social settings. Our reality is therefore socially constructed. If we can shift the construction, we alter the meaning and if we alter the meaning we change the experience. Therefore the views of the subject have to be sought and understood. In appreciating the other's meaning, the social worker helps the client recognize, value and own their experience. This produces authenticity which should lead to the client recovering responsibility for his own actions. In practice, this flavours each phase of the social work process in a distinctive subjective way.

**Defining the problem: a problem for me or a problem for you?**
Writers in this field are prone to ask the big questions in life: Who are you? What is going on? What does it all mean? Clients are people who are anxious about their identity and purpose. These 'existential' problems create anxiety and these anxieties usually occur in reference to other people – husbands, children, friends. It is therefore most important to discover how the client defines the *problem*, what it means to him and what he has tried to do about it, if anything. The

concept of problem, then, helps the social worker become more sensitive to the client's actual and current 'state of being' (Goldstein 1984, pp.282–3). For many clients, particularly those seeking counsel, there is a need simply to recognize and to articulate what ails them. Just talking to a sympathetic ear does wonders. Of course, this may well be a prerequisite to doing something about it, but it is most important for the individual to explore and eventually locate the trouble as he or she sees it.

The concept of self is that of a potentially purposeful, reflective and self-determining body. People 'are capable of redefining and resolving the obstacles that block the path toward a more rewarding and confirming existence' (ibid., p.5). In the approach of the humanist, half the battle is to enable the client to face up to the true nature and proportion of his difficulties. If this is achieved, he is well placed to attempt the next stage. At this point he maps out his choices. Having chosen, he unequivocally assumes responsibility for the direction in which he is about to take himself.

It has to be noted that throughout client-centred practices, in marked contrast to the material determinism which we shall meet in Marxist welfare work, the responsibility for change lies with the individual. 'Man is nothing else but that which he makes himself. This is the first principle of existentialism' (Sartre in Kaufman 1957, p.289). The existential challenge is for him to take hold of his own life and impose meaning on it. He needs purpose. He must not allow himself to become passive, tossed helplessly about by events. This would be a case of bad faith. It is within everyone's power to assume control over their lives. It is up to social workers to help them do this.

Interactionists argue slightly differently. They see that for many clients the experience of being labelled a problem is itself part of the problem. Whenever someone is referred to a social worker as a problem, the worker should retort, 'Problem? Says who?' What is it about the client's behaviour that causes other people, usually in a position of relative power *vis-à-vis* the client, to describe them as delinquent, mentally ill or dangerous? It is critical for the interactionist to be clear how things look to key participants: what does the client and his behaviour mean to his parents, the police, the school, the courts, the Social Services Department and above all to the client himself? At the end of this exploration, a profile of the problem and what it means to those involved should emerge. What also should become clear is what each participant expects to happen. The social worker often finds herself at the centre of a web of conflicting demands. She needs to be absolutely clear who is expecting what of whom.

## Explanation and assessment: understanding experience

There are two aspects to be noted about the assessment phase for those whose theoretical roots lie in this paradigm. The first is straightforward. The worker must be alert to the process by which problems become identified, maintained and even amplified and how this is experienced by the client. The second is a question of how information is gathered which allows such explanations. The subjectivist needs to know her subject: so the assessment process must ensure that the client's position is understood. Halfpenny's (1979) description of 'interpretivism' is a help:

> In the interpretivist approach 'understanding' the actions and interactions of respondents, by virtue of grasping and comprehending the culturally appropriate concepts through which they conduct their social life is the way in which explanation is achieved (p.808).

Unlike the scientific practitioners who approach their clients in an object-to-object model, interactionists define themselves in a subject-to-subject relation to their clients. Knowledge is gained through participation, not detached observation. Denzin (1970) gives clear advice to those who wish to be interactionists, which transfers well to social work. The assessor should strive to see the client's point of view. She should enter into and attempt to fathom the subjective world of the client. She should show how meanings arise in the context of behaviour. Whenever possible, the social worker should gather her observations in 'naturally-occurring' situations -- in the home, the school, the youth club. The social worker claims no superior knowledge. She values the account of events given by her clients. This is her starting point. The aim is to understand the experience of others, to respect them and to believe that a true appreciation of the other's point of view is the only basis for a humanistic practice. The social worker is intent on understanding how the client sees himself and defines his situation. All this is in contrast to the scientific, positivist approaches which seek to explain behaviour, to predict it and thereby control it.

The assessment should be able to describe the problem and more importantly say for whom it is a problem. It should be able to examine the context in which the 'problem' or 'need' takes on its meaning as well as consider whether difficulties are sustained by such acts as labelling. It should judge whether the difficulties lie with the person who sees the problem or the person seen as a problem.

By the end of the assessment stage, the client and the social worker, together, should be able to answer most of the following questions: What is the matter? Why now? How has it come about? What have you tried to do about it? How do other people behave towards you and your problem? How does this behaviour affect you? Finally, what is to be done?

## Aims: creating new meanings

In general terms, the aim is to produce a greater understanding between all participants so that clashes in perceptions and expectations are reduced. If everyone can begin to agree what the situation means, there is less room for confusion, less opportunity to project and fantasize about the other. In practice, this often entails a preparedness to redefine the problem and the machinery that handles that problem. If the definitions change, so do the interpretations and responses available. Interactionists, for example, are keen to change the 'process' and not the person. If being chewed over by the relentless machinery of the legal process serves only to amplify a person's deviant ways, then it seems only sensible to change the machinery of the legal process.

Humanists are generally against the concept of treatment; doing something to someone. If anything is to be done, it should be done together. Diagnoses become shared assessments. Thus we have what has been termed the 'non-treatment paradigm' (Bottoms and McWilliams 1979). The aim is to help, not to cure.

## Methods: the communication of understanding

So how are such aims achieved? Again, Whittington and Holland (1985) offer a sharp summary, although they do tend to confuse assessment, aims and methods:

> Different expectations and problem definitions should be clarified, communication improved, confusion reduced. Clients' unheard or ill-expressed versions of problems should be represented. Key labellers should be identified; dubious, premature or harmful labels challenged; and problem definitions renegotiated (p.39).

Sometimes with the individual, more often in groups, the social worker helps clients realize how labels and identities have become attached to their way of doing things. An important strategy is to divert clients away from 'deviant careers'. Alternatives to prison and psychiatric hospital are developed. Children should be kept out of courts. More ambitiously, social workers should fight against prejudice wherever and whenever it works against the old or mentally handicapped, black teenagers or single mothers. Most social work clients feel stigmatized. The public has to be educated in its attitudes towards those groups who are liable to suffer the blemish of stigma. The labelled and the labellers are encouraged to speak to one another in the hope that mutual understanding leads to a less rigid, less institutionalized response, otherwise both remain locked in a downhill tumble of mutually hostile attitudes. The approach 'underscores the need to be certain that the people who may be beneficiaries of such projects are active participants and decision-makers in the process' (Goldstein 1984, p.xii).

Some of the best examples of practice of this type is in the area of 'alternatives to custody'. (See, for example, Pointing 1986.) Delinquent adolescents, who might normally be destined for detention centre or residential care, are steered away from the damaging experience of closed institutional living. Instead of being 'sent away' they remain at home though they must attend whatever day-time and evening schemes are taking the place of the custodial sentence. Not only is the 'alternative' non-custodial, it is designed to provide a useful, constructive experience. The young adolescent may learn to maintain a motor-bike or repair the damage of local vandals. He or she may develop skills in cooking or become expert in carpentry. The group itself offers support, advice and insight. Working together teaches co-operation and promotes self-esteem. Whereas detention centres only make matters worse, alternatives to custody aim to recover those who are rapidly slipping beyond the sympathies of the host society.

Such schemes require much liaison and co-operation with local magistrates and the groundwork prior to launching a project demands strong and sensitive political skills on the part of the workers. In their social enquiry reports, social workers must argue that it is better to keep adolescents out of custody and that a community-based sentence is more appropriate. Magistrates seem to be impressed with alternatives that hint at compensation and reparation by the offender. As Allen (1986) puts it:

> If the magistrates' aim is . . . to teach the young offender to live freely in the community without indulging in unacceptable behaviour, it is up to social workers to show that such teaching is far more effective in the community (p.26).

Removal to a place of supervised custody is no help whatsoever in achieving this aim.

Still in the area of working with offenders, Adams (1985) offers a neat example from the world of intermediate treatment (IT). He contrasts two actual workers and their two very different styles of practice: one based on 'truth', the other based on 'love'.

In our terms, the first is set firmly within the objective, scientific mood of functionalism. It is a rational approach, emphasizing reason and the need to plan and order practice. Over the years IT workers have been encouraged to think clearly and act logically. Objectives are set and methods devised. Everything's done for a purpose and the purpose is explicitly stated. Group activities are 'the means to the ultimate end of reducing the likelihood of boys offending in the future' (ibid., p.399). 'Treatment' programmes are run along systematic lines in a task-orientated climate as the way to cure wrongdoing. This is the way of 'truth'.

The second version has all the ingredients of thorough-going subjectivism. Here, the proper nature of IT is taken to be that of 'an experience'. The way the group travels is far more important than planning its final destination. So, records Adams, 'asked about the evaluation of an IT programme, one social worker claimed "a good time was had by all" as an outcome more legitimate than any impact on the behaviour of young people participating' (ibid., p.393). Whereas the boys in the rationally formulated programme follow the direction and purposes of the project leader, the worker in the 'experiential' model follows the wishes and inclinations of the boys. Things just happen and this is good. It is what the boys want. They develop ideas and activities that suit them. The worker merely facilitates. He listens and accepts. He is intuitive. Expression is valued more than purpose. This is the way of 'love'.

This last illustration wades into a client-centred practice. In fact, for our main example we shall return to these person-centred approaches. They represent an important tradition in social work. Their appeal to practitioners appears as strong as ever. The next chapter, therefore, is devoted to an exegesis of their philosophy and practice. They like to paint in strong colours and have little time for the mannered designs of their more technical cousins.

# 11 Client-Centred Approaches

## The natural psychologist

We are all natural psychologists. Indeed, believes Humphrey (1986), human beings have an in-built aptitude for doing psychology. It is not just a clever thing to be able to do. It is a basic and necessary social skill given the sort of creatures that we are. The very size of our large skulls, claims Humphrey, is accounted for by the brain power that is required to do natural psychology. Now just in case this is beginning to sound a little removed from the humanistic leanings that we outlined in the last chapter, let me explain why the work of Humphrey offers an apt beginning to the client-centred approach.

It all starts with gorillas. Why should these animals, with their relatively easy-going life style, have such large brains? Humphrey went to the jungle and pondered. It seemed to him that, although the forest itself may not present any great survival problems to gorillas, the behaviour of other gorillas can and does. The intelligence required to survive socially is of quite a different order to that needed to seek food and cope with the jungle:

> Social intelligence is clearly the key to the great apes' biological success. It is in dealing with each other that these animals have to think, remember, calculate, and weigh things up inside their heads. And social intelligence requires every ounce of brain power they have got (ibid., p.39).

It seemed to Humphrey that gorillas and chimps had evolved to be psychologists by nature: they were natural psychologists, attuned to handle their relationships with one another. What is true for the apes is certainly true for human beings. People evolved to be psychologists by nature. In order to survive, people need to do psychology, they need social intelligence, an awareness of the moods, intentions and reactions of other people. Human beings, believes Humphrey, are supremely good at understanding one another. How is this done? What is this ability to read other people's minds, anticipate their reactions and put ourselves in their shoes? The answer is the 'inner eye'.

When we watch other people, we do not see a random or arbitrary set of actions. We see a causal structure underpinning their movements. We observe plans, emotions, memories. We sense what they are up to and why. However, the ability to do this rests on the ability to observe and be aware of our own thought processes. It is as if we each have an 'inner eye' which looks at the brain and sees why and how it is we are acting in the way that we are. It is a consciousness of self, a self-consciousness. What would the possession of such a brain mechanism do for our ability to be psychologists?

> To begin with, it would mean that each individual human being would have almost literally a headstart in reading his own mind. No more fussing about like a behaviourist psychologist with 'intelligent guesses' about what lies behind our own behaviour. We would know immediately where the deeper explanation lies — in our own brain-states, which our inner eye reveals. But in practice it would mean very much more: for the explanation we have of our own behaviour could then form the basis for explaining *other people's*, too. We could, in effect, imagine what it's like to be them, because we know what it's like to be ourselves (ibid., p.71).

This is an intriguing line of support for those who believe that, naturally, we can tune into the thoughts and feelings of others, that intuition is a quality that people possess. It is certainly a view of human beings that finds favour with many social workers. Although 'humanism' has a long history in social work, reaching something of an apotheosis in the writing of Biestek (1961), we shall turn to the work of three recent authors to give us some idea of the current state of the social worker as humanist.

**Words of love**
The authors and their three books cover common ground but in different styles. One is eloquent and cultured (England 1986). Another is worthy and sincere (Goldstein 1984). The third is spirited and uncompromising (Wilkes 1981). However, like all writing in this area, they have a vocabulary in common. In fact, they can be recognized by the words they use. So, given an interest in the other person and her subjective experience, it is not surprising to find social workers being 'person-centred' and empathetic. They have and use 'intuition'. They show 'love' and 'respect'. Feelings are shared. The touchstone of true reality is experience. Therefore 'experiential' learning is the only worthwhile learning. Good social work is described as 'creative', more like an 'art' and less like a science.

In some varieties, social workers are keen to emphasize the equality of the relationship with the client. They do not come as expert technicians, skilled in fixing broken psyches. Their practice is non-judgemental, non-directive and accepts the other unconditionally. They come as fellow-travellers, willing to spend time exploring with the other person 'where they are at and where they are going', usually in the 'here and now'. Instead of treating or changing, social workers prefer to talk of helping. Goldstein, for example, writes of the helping process as a creative experience both for the worker and the client. Help does not start with the worker's private assumptions about what is wrong. Indeed, the vulnerable client is offered 'a measure of security and respect – and, at the very least, a promise that his or her life will not be meddled with' (Goldstein 1984, p.278). 'Love of one's neighbour,' believes Wilkes (1981, p.61), 'applies to all, by virtue of one's common humanity, and no exceptions are permitted.' Good social workers, echoes England (1986, p.136), are moved by a loving interest in their fellow men. They offer trust and concern.

All of this makes stringent demands on the *person* of the worker. This is why a deliberate use, understanding and appreciation of self is basic to any worthwhile social work practice. Social work practice, states Brandon (1979, p.30), another humanist, 'concerns who we are rather than what we may know'. Mind you, there is always the danger for some that 'person-centred' becomes 'self-centred'. 'Let's talk' is liable to degenerate into 'let's talk about me'. There is always a suspicion of sanctimony in those who say that they are in touch with themselves. In his critical and witty examination of the new psychotherapies, Clare (1981) notes the ever-present threat to those who wish to understand self to become seekers of self in what amounts to blind egoism. By way of a warning, he quotes from a poster hanging on the wall of a Californian growth centre:

> I do my thing, you do your thing. I am not in this world to live up to your expectations and you are not in this world to live up to mine! You are you, and I am I, and if by chance we meet, it's beautiful, if not, it can't be helped (ibid., p.226).

Now I am not sure that I am choosing the following quote by Brandon with entire fairness. However, he did write it and it does seem to exemplify what happens when Clare's cautionary tale is ignored: 'For me,' says Brandon (1979, p.34), 'social work is essentially a pilgrimage. It is a journey concerned with helping myself rather than others, a way of more fully knowing myself.' That for a social worker does seem to be going too far.

### The critique of social work as an applied social science

The social sciences, in emulating the natural sciences, seek to reduce human behaviour to a bundle of constituent parts. There is a wish to identify mechanisms which account for the things we do and say. However, according to those with a humanistic and subjectivistic outlook, this is no way to understand human beings. People are always so much more than the sum of their parts.

Even so, social work has turned to the social sciences, particularly psychology, for accounts of human behaviour which can be applied in practice. There are several reasons why this might be. One is a need for certainty, a wish to tie down those things which are all too fluid in human affairs. Another is the demand that social work proves itself. This tends to mean that the occupation should demonstrate its effectiveness in matters such as stopping delinquents misbehaving or curing families of their inadequacies. In turn this calls for measurements, yardsticks by which to judge whether teenagers have changed their ways or families have been cured of their social shortcomings. Measuring people reduces them to a limited number of quantifiable dimensions. If this is how social work is to be judged and it wants to play its part, then it has to look to science and its ways if it is going to offer even a glimpse of a measurable performance.

> A belief that the only reliable knowledge is that obtained by the scientific method results in a goal-oriented social work where the outcomes are judged in terms of concrete, behavioural change. The approach is impersonal, non-involved, calculating, interfering, and expert. The helper does not become involved with the person he or she is trying to help and the question of self-knowledge does not arise. The self cannot be observed . . . nor can it be measured, so it must be ignored . . . A certain result is expected and, since it must be measurable in terms of behaviour, anything inward-looking is excluded from the start. In a managerial society it is difficult to justify social work activity except in terms of results (Wilkes 1981, p.75).

As appliers of science, social workers want to explain — but they will not understand. They use their heads but know nothing of the heart. They emphasize activity, having a preference for 'doing' rather than 'being'. Tasks are set without ever stopping to find out what just living and being is all about. Wilkes points out that clinicians, like humanists, have their own language. They have a fondness for diagnosing, treating and changing. Practice of this kind is positivist, objective and utilitarian. It turns social work into a branch of technology.

However, in practice, the social worker as applied scientist can only handle topics which are simple and amenable. She looks for those situations that allow her to flex her technological muscles whilst ignoring the less tangible issues. 'We thus have precise knowledge of what is not worth knowing' (Rickman quoted in England 1986, p.79). All of which confirms the established research evidence that social workers and therapists work best in cases which need them least. Some human problems have no solution. Sympathy is more important than ideology. Without compassion, social work is empty. Science provides no answers, 'there can never be an adequate material description of social work' (England 1986, p.8).

## A humanist practice

Throughout these chapters I am making the case that the assumptions held about people and society which underlie each paradigm affect every stage of practice in ways peculiar and distinctive to that paradigm. The humanist's thinking and practice is no exception. There is a consistency that runs as a thread through every aspect of the work. It goes something like this.

People are not like machines and the way in which we understand people is not like the way in which we understand machines. There can be no science of knowing people. In fact, we have to learn how to see people from the inside. Understanding does not come from looking at them objectively, from the outside. What we have is a natural ability, if we allow it, to appreciate the thoughts and feelings of others. In short, we have intuition. When social workers meet clients, all they have is their selves, their intuition and a relationship. An awareness of self and an understanding of how the self affects relationships are fundamental to good social work. It is in relationship with another person that we strive, together, to make sense of what is going on, to interpret what we find and to discover meaning in what we do and what we are. In order for all this to happen, social workers must be able to *communicate* – to communicate what they know and feel, what they hear, what they think and understand and what it might mean.

Practice in this style requires the social worker to approach the client with respect, dignity and equality. She is an explorer of meaning. She shows 'a commitment to the client's subjective world' (Goldstein 1986, p.355). As might be guessed from the account offered, it is difficult to capture examples of good, vivid practice in print, although our chosen proponents do attempt the task. What we shall do here is develop further the essential character of a humanistic practice before finally offering a brief description of an actual piece of work.

## The art of helping

> A recently qualified social worker visited a man who was dying from cancer and returned without seeing him. The patient's wife had said there were no problems and as the man was dying there seemed to the social worker to be no point in seeing him. There was no target to hit, no plan to implement. There was nothing to be done. The possibility that the establishment of human contact and the recognition that, although dying, the man was a human being who mattered were both more important than achieving positive results did not occur to the student. He had not been trained to think that way, but rather to look for a purpose and, thus, no other way of putting things had ever occurred to him (Wilkes 1981, pp.92–3).

Well, that is how not to do it. The whole of Wilkes's book is written as a protest against a way of thinking that seeks to control and change life. In its place she offers a way of helping. The idea is not to shape or mend another's behaviour but to understand it from their point of view, to say 'what are you going through; I would like to understand'. It is an approach that calls for humility and patience, 'an attitude of respect towards the world and an awareness of its infinite mystery and complexity' (ibid., p.88). Social workers should not meddle. They should develop an attitude of 'non-possessive concern', which leaves a person free to change in their own way or, if it is his wish, not to change at all. The approach is expressive and descriptive rather than purposive and explanatory. It is in this spirit that Wilkes ends her book with the following advice to the aspiring social worker, 'do not explain, do not try to change, but just look'. We started this section with an example of how not to be helpful. We end with a quote from Jordan's (1979) highly personal account of helping, and in this instance what he finds helpful:

> In my experience, the kind of person who helps me be truthful, who helps me get to the point of looking at the conflicts which are disabling me, is someone who is real and credible as a person himself. His responses are real, from the whole of himself. Even if he is wrong, or misunderstands me, he rings true, because he is saying what is real for him . . . if he comments on what I have told him, it will not be just for the sake of being clever, or giving my 'problems' some new objective quality. He won't turn my difficulties into things, give them labels, wrap them up neatly in his ideas. He will share my real feelings with me when he thinks mine are distorted, and when he thinks I'm not being straight . . . Very often through him I will see that there are much deeper implications in the things that were bothering me than I realised before. But this will not be through his smart interpretations, but through the real wisdom that allows me to follow my own processes of thought. Somehow, without knowing why, I shall feel better after I've talked to him because I shall not have escaped from anything, or twisted anything. I shan't have been reassured or cosseted or treated like a child, but I shall have been recognised, treated as real, by a fellow human being (pp.25–6).

## Intuition

As we have said, men and women are natural psychologists. We learn about each other, not through reading textbooks, but naturally, intuitively. Through our imaginations and innate ability to resonate with the experiences of the other, we can create our own picture of the client's world. For England, intuition is the essence of social work. Social workers very often annoy and mystify their critics, he says, because they explain their practice with such terms as 'I just knew that was how they felt'. But this is just how it is. Social workers, like other people, often do just know. No amount of insistence that they prove or materially demonstrate this knowledge can alter this fact. Subjective knowledge is 'not a knowledge about, but a direct awareness of life, direct communication, direct awakening, seeing people as they really are' (Brandon 1979, p.19). It is an altogether 'softer' kind of knowledge, born of experience, born of the imagination and the worker's intuitive use of self.

### Use of self and the relationship

The reference point for an understanding of others is one's self. Jordan (1979, p.26) says that helping is not simply a skill or a technique. Helping is a test of the helper as a person. To help her clients, the social worker must be able to make imaginative use of her own experience, particularly as it occurs in the immediate relationship. The 'use of self' defines both the social worker's practice knowledge and her practice behaviour. The worker must be aware of her own thoughts and emotions; if she feels hostile or protective towards the client, she must know this, note it and be prepared to use it. Seligman's introduction to her work is typical of the style, which sees itself as personal and creative, 'in this chapter my aims are to describe who I am, and to say what I do and how I feel about it and how my "clients" react to me and my work' (in Brandon and Jordan 1979, p.114).

This intuitive feel of the other person and the effect on oneself produces an understanding which becomes an integral part of the worker's self. Thus, the worker gains her understanding, not by a struggle to explore external issues, but by articulating her own consciousness. England (1986, p.35) believes that 'a pervasive use of self is the crucial centre point of social work'. It is this deliberate recognition of how we are experiencing and understanding what is happening, as it happens, that has to be used, sensitively and imaginatively, in the relationship that creates those very thoughts and feelings. Subjectivity – one's own as well as the other person's – is the touchstone of human understanding. To know oneself is to know the other and to know the other is to know oneself.

Such understanding is peculiar to the people involved. It is part of their relationship. And it is within successful helping relationships that we encounter the qualities of empathy, genuineness and warmth, which in themselves are often said to be sufficient for those seeking help. They ask no more. To be understood and not judged is enough. If nothing else, social workers should be able to 'relate' to people. The social worker, believes Wiegard (mentioned in England 1986, p.46), is like the sculptor who frees the sculpted form from the marble; the worker recognizes the potential of the client and enables him to realize that potential. On this basis might social work be compared to creative art.

## Meaning and interpretation

We are now at the core of the humanist's practice. The search for meaning — in events, in life, in relation with other people — is the existential quest that lies behind the problems in living met by social workers and experienced by clients. What we make of life depends on how we define it (Goldstein 1984, p.28). Social workers have to stop, listen — listen very hard — and search for the meanings that guide actions, influence thoughts and colour emotions. We all try to make sense out of living. The client wants to be understood, he wants the social worker to know what he means, how he interprets the world in which he lives. This requires an intensely *personal* service:

> That social workers will need to know about the meaning of experience is the only constant and the only necessary element in all social work accounts. Social work is always about the way in which people see things, and it is a personal service because perception is always unique. Any account of social work must therefore be based upon an account of perception, for social work is based upon the meaning people give to their experience (England 1986, p.17).

Throughout all the accounts, social work is identified as a process of understanding the meaning which people give to their experience. It is the notion of meaning which gives the human studies their distinctive character. It is 'the perceiving self', of both the worker and the client, that is the focus of good practice. The approach is thoroughly subjective. It is the only way to understand human behaviour. So, for example, writes Rickman (quoted in England 1986):

> We cannot know why a person becomes a delinquent without understanding his fears, ambitions and interests . . . They are subjective in that they are always the states of a subject, what somebody feels, how somebody experiences a situation and how somebody sees the world . . . We are dealing with interpretations of reality (p.80).

Quite clearly, given the tenor of the subjectivist's method, the search for meaning is a shared endeavour; 'sometimes,' add Brandon and Jordan (1979, pp.3—4), 'to the point where there is a kind of fusion between client and social worker'. It is a reflective process. It is a collaborative venture as the client considers the meanings that inform his existence and seeks to reconstruct a better reality.

> The process grants the client responsibility for explaining his or her predicament, for participating in how the predicament is

defined, and for determining solutions to it . . . The client also determines the helper's role in achieving these ends . . . the process involves the client in new and possibly more productive ways of reasoning about his or her problem — the most vital aspect of the helping experience (Goldstein 1986, p.355).

## Communicating understanding

Of course, all this understanding and fathoming of meaning counts for nothing unless it is communicated and mutually recognized. However, what is communicated and how is it done? There are few guidelines, no formulae for what we say, except, says Brandon (1979, p.31), that our words and actions come from the heart rather than the head. Again, quite what this actually means in practice is not quite clear. All three of our authors consider the matter. Goldstein offers his usual measured treatment, Wilkes her characteristic passionate response. But for me, the most sparkling and original address to the business of communicating and understanding is given by England. He mixes a powerful blend of communication, art and criticism for social work practice. In turn, he is inspired by the writing of Raymond Williams and makes particular use of *The Long Revolution* (1965). Here is what England and Williams say on the matter of successful communication.

Each of us is constantly constructing an understanding of the world. However, it is only in the act of communication itself that the understanding is formulated. 'The process of communication is the process of finding common meaning . . . The meaning must be communicated to be realized' (England 1986, p.110). The experience of others not only has to be recognized but that recognition communicated. It is good to feel understood. It confirms the experience:

> It is . . . to everyman a matter of urgent personal importance to 'describe' his experience, because this is literally a remaking of himself, a creative change in his personal organisation . . . [The] impulse to communicate is a learned human response to disturbance of any kind. For the individual of course the struggle is to communicate successfully by describing adequately . . . unless the description is adequate, there can be no relevant communication (Williams 1965, p.42).

This makes it quite clear that communication is a reciprocal activity; it includes reception and response. If successful, it leads to a shared understanding of experience and what it means. It is through communicating that we are able to make sense of our own experience. In this very simple sense, just talking and listening are extremely important elements in the practice of social work. Any technological overlay or expert imposition interferes with this process, leading to frustrated clients and poor practice. Being good phenomenologists, both Williams and England argue that people actively create their understanding of the world and its ways. Description, through communication, is an essential part in the achievement of understanding. Fundamentally:

> Each person's ability to make sense, and to organize an understanding of the world, depends upon the ability to communicate about that understanding. 'Reality' is only maintained by its communication and such communication is particularly urgent at times of stress (England 1986, p.112).

At this stage, we need to recognize that all this is also a description of what an artist does. Creativity in art is the process and the means of sharing understanding. The artist is someone possessed of particular skills. She can do two very important things. She can get inside and understand an experience; and she can express and communicate that experience in a way that allows others also to understand that experience. The insights of the creative artist help find and organize new descriptions of experience which are then transmitted to others. It is the role of the artist to be skilled in helping others experience meanings. If social workers are people who help others understand their experience and find meaning, then social workers are artists.

We can now appreciate the strength of England's assertions as he develops his theme: 'The task of the social worker,' he says, 'is always to understand the meaning of experience and to communicate that understanding' (ibid., p.21), 'but,' he adds later, 'the construction and communication of that understanding are possible only through the worker's own meaning, only through the way in which the worker himself sees the world' (ibid., p.32). Good social work, it is claimed, requires of the workers an ability to be very aware of themselves, their immediate personal experience and the skill to communicate that awareness. 'The worker must know his client's problem almost as if he were living it, and *show* his knowledge' (ibid., p.23).

The final strand promotes the idea of the social worker as critic as well as artist. As they communicate meaning, social workers 'create'. However, they also evaluate as they weigh up and critically assess those communications. 'The social worker has to be particularly skilled at the evaluation, or understanding of his client's meaning and is thus his client's critic' (ibid., p.119). The social worker is also a critic of his own performance. Such descriptions produce 'stories' about the client and the social worker. These stories should be evocative and reflective, searching and critical. So, chimes Goldstein (1984) in language not quite possessing the cadence of his English counterpart:

> Respecting the client's frame of reference invites the client to tell his or her story; as the story unfolds, the helper, in the Socratic sense, raises questions the client could not ask himself or herself; and the answers lead to yet other questions which

open new cognitive pathways of understanding. What we call redefining reality or concept-learning directs attention to the reflective and thought processes by which one can make better sense of one's life and experience (p.294).

## Making sense for good practice

As practice in this manner relies on intuition, the use of self, the quality of the relationship, the understanding of experience, the search for meaning and the communication of these understandings, we should not be too surprised to discover that written accounts somehow fail to do justice to the full intensity that characterizes work of this kind at its best. Nor do we find a neat, clear sequence of problem, assessment, aims and method. In particular, there is an inclination to conflate the problem and the assessment. This is necessarily so. It is the client who is best placed to articulate his condition and consider what it means for him. It is the client's view that has to be identified, explored and understood.

The *aim*, however, is quite distinct. The social worker should help the client recognize and realize his experience and understand what it means for him. If understanding changes, so does meaning, and if meaning changes so does the perception of the experience. Perceptions, therefore, can be altered and extended (England 1986, p.7; Goldstein 1984, p.45). The way a battered wife views herself or the outlook which a terminally ill patient has on her condition may shift as the situation and what it means is reconstructed.

Such changes are achieved in the act of understanding which takes place as the worker and client reflect on experiences, search for meaning and strive to communicate what it is they have come to know and understand. This is the method – and a personally demanding one it is too. The quality of understanding is a product of the quality of the relationship.

## Brian and Vicky, Claire and a social worker

The following example is given by one of England's students; but first, a qualification.

A good social work report, we are advised, should tell a story, a story about the client and a story about the worker. In the story, the description should be full, evocative, critical and reflective. We should read of thoughts raised, feelings stirred, understandings shared. Unfortunately, I shall not be telling a very good story, partly because I offer a précis, partly because the description is shorn of its detail and colour and partly because it is second-hand. By definition I cannot offer a very fair or appropriate account of this social worker's practice, at least in the terms demanded by the strictures of creative practice. I raid the body of the story and give the bare bones of a tale, a mere skeleton, There is little form, no shape, scant movement, not a smile nor a frown struggle through, no sense of the real hopes and fears. The full text really has to be read (England 1986, pp.180—94). However, I shall take a deep breath and press on, and hope that this extract stimulates an interest in the more substantial piece itself.

Four years ago, at the age of twenty-two, Mrs Claire W. was diagnosed as having a wasting, debilitating disease of the bowel. This condition had caused her to become very infirm. An earlier referral said that there was concern that Mrs W. was neglecting to care for herself and her house, with an indication that this might have been having a detrimental effect on her marriage.

More recently, Mrs W.'s GP contacted the Social Services Department to say that Mrs W. was giving serious consideration to having a baby. The GP felt worried as Mrs W. now requires a great deal of attention herself. 'It was agreed that Mrs W. may need skilled counselling in this matter.'

Things were further complicated when it was learned from the GP, six weeks later, that Vicky, a thirteen-year-old girl, had been visiting the home regularly at Mr Brian W.'s invitation to do odd jobs:

> There was no suggestion of improper behaviour. However, Mrs W. was due to go into hospital for a fortnight's rest, and the GP (whose own marriage had recently broken down) expressed anxiety about what might happen if Mr W. got into trouble over Vicky, and subsequently could not look after his wife.

A number of worries and problems were becoming clearly recognizable. Claire was dependent and unhappy. The marriage was none too good. Claire was concerned about Vicky, who was not only getting into trouble with the police, but appeared to have a crush on Brian. 'Claire', writes the social worker, 'was feeling jealous, hurt and powerless.' Much of this unhappiness is detected intuitively by the worker. She 'picks up' Claire's worries about the marriage. She uses her imagination and senses how Claire must see things, and how she must feel as a highly dependent person, a 'failed' wife, and a hurt, jealous woman. In the account, the worker describes events in a sensitive, thoughtful style.

At first, the social worker speculates about the situation. Her assessment is based on various intuitions, but she needs to check them out with Claire and Brian. Is Claire a victim of people who want to control her life, or does she have a passive personality? Is this the way she copes with her disability? The worker began to feel that the disease meant Claire had 'suffered a loss of her role as a wife in the traditional sense, and also her image as a woman'. Her husband seemed to find it difficult to adjust to the realities of his wife's disease.

England, in his discussion of this work, feels that the worker's goals remained a little obscure. Nevertheless, it is apparent what she is trying to do. She is helping Claire explore what is happening, she wants Claire to realize her difficult experiences, and she directs their joint efforts towards establishing a reconstruction of the way in which Claire must see the world. This last aim is a pre-requisite if Claire is to identify a set of meanings in her life which makes her less dependent, more of a 'fighter' and ultimately more happy. So we hear the social worker say that her 'role was to help Claire maintain her own sense of integrity' and to give her 'a chance to come to terms with her disability'.

The social worker meets Claire and Brian and they talk. It is a method which sees the worker trying to help Claire and Brian understand what is happening. She relies a good deal on what she senses is being experienced and she seeks to communicate this understanding to the husband and wife. In this way, she hopes to help them articulate, clarify and accept their experiences. Holding a clearer view of their world, they should then be in a position to make better sense of what is happening and so be able to do something about it.

They begin to talk more honestly, but it brings pain. It is eventually agreed that the worker will meet Claire alone:

> Claire wanted Vicky not to visit any more . . . I maintained an impartial and clarifying role, Brian began to state his point of view more explicitly. He said that he had always wanted children, and he enjoyed Vicky's company. He felt that Claire's illness had deprived him of fatherhood, and that now he had a right to enjoy children's company. He felt that Claire was jealously mistrusting him and he wanted her to have faith in his integrity. He saw it as a test of the marriage. Claire in her turn began to express feelings of hurt, and said that if she wasn't ill she would go and find a boyfriend for herself. I came away feeling that Brian and Claire were treading very carefully with each other's feelings . . . Brian would not admit that he fancied Vicky and not Claire, and Claire did not admit the extent of her hurt. They seemed to have reached a precarious stalemate (ibid., pp.189–90).

What has happened is that in this initial phase the worker has established a good, albeit painful description of what is being perceived, experienced and understood. In the final stages, the social worker creates a more constructive interpretation of Claire's situation in which she can identify who she is and where she can and might go.

As Claire and the worker progress, it becomes apparent to Claire that she must distance herself from her husband if she is to survive. The social worker feels sad for Claire but senses that the woman is brave and capable. Claire picks up that the worker believes in her inner strengths and is encouraged. The worker continues to help Claire express her feelings and 'explore ways of increasing her self-esteem by lowering her dependence on Brian'. Claire gradually senses that, if she is to maintain her own integrity, she has to fight Brian and the situation in which she finds herself.

By the end of the account, Claire has begun to change. She is learning to experience her world in a different way. Claire is a little more independent, but her difficult physical and emotional position still make her feel fragile. The worker concludes:

> Claire no longer talks about how to cope with Vicky as she knows she copes very well with her . . . Neither does she express a longing to have a baby. She is looking after herself first, and seeing this as her first priority (ibid.).

Commenting on this report, England congratulates the social worker for maintaining an effective balance between analysis (the social worker as critic) and evocation (the social worker as artist):

> [The] strength of the account lies always not simply in its vital portrayal of the client's experience, but in the vitality of the portrayal of the social worker's relevant experience. It makes it clear that it is only through reporting her consciousness that the worker can give plausible life to her account of others. It makes it clear that to know of the worker's knowledge and action we must know of the worker herself (ibid., p.200).

# 12 The Raisers of Consciousness

**Radical humanism**

The mixture here is one of humanism and politics. An appreciation of the individual's subjective condition is sharply set within a picture of a society in conflict. Similar to those who seek meaning, the radical humanist sees the individual creating the world in which she lives. However, for the radical humanist, this world is a fraught place, full of inequities. The nature of society and the state of the individual's consciousness are critically related.

Examination of this relationship leads to a radical critique of society, particularly as it affects people's state of mind. Many of the problems people experience, personally, psychologically and socially, can only be understood in terms of the dehumanizing characteristics of modern society. Not content just to savour the subjective quality of social life, the radical humanist is intent on doing something about it. Her wish is to release the full potential of the human spirit, freeing it from the distorting effects of the manifold social iniquities inherent in a capitalist system.

It will be evident from what has been said that the two dimensions of the subjective and the objective, and the individual's consciousness and his society, bear on each other intimately. Perhaps more than any other, the radical humanist wilfully and necessarily has to explore the mutual impact of the subjectivity on the individual and his society. To talk of one is to describe the condition of the other. Of course, put like this it remains overly cryptic. It needs elaboration, particularly as the forms of practice that emerge out of the paradigm lead to a distinct focus on freeing the human mind as a pre-requisite for changing society, which is to say humanize it, a place fit for human beings.

There is something about society, markedly so since the industrial revolution, that limits the potentialities of its members. In his earlier writings, Marx described a society which he saw dominating the lives of people in every facet. Their experience was torn in two by a system that treated people as just part of the machinery of creating capital. People became alienated from their work and, to the extent that other people were no more than cogs in the wheel, alienated from each other. The creation of a system of production which regards people as no more than means to an impersonal, inhuman end – the accumulation of capital – causes a profound split in the relationship between the subjective world of men and women and the objective world they create but which comes to oppress and dominate them and their minds.

Theorists who go exploring in the paradigm have identified a number of forms of alienation. Each form inhibits the full possibilities of human potential. Burrell and Morgan (1979) mention four, each associated with a particular author:

1  The reification of society (Georg Lukacs).
2  The notion of ideological hegemony (Antonio Gramsci).
3  The idea of one-dimensional man (Herbert Marcuse).
4  The pathology of communication (Jurgen Habermas).

Between them they cover some heavy intellectual ground. Each one describes men and women as alienated from the objective, external world which nevertheless is of our own making. For this we pay a heavy psychological price. If we do not feel at home in the world created by men and women, then we are strangers in our own land. Society is the product of the minds of human beings and yet it takes on an apparent objective life of its own, even though it is made of subjective projections. In this way, society, which is an abstract concept, is experienced as a real, concrete thing. It is reified. Marx, for example:

> Saw the society of his day as dominating human experience; objectified social creations reflected back upon man as an alienating force, dominating his essential being and nature (Burrell and Morgan 1979, pp.281–2).

If people feel that society oppresses and dominates them, they live only half a life. They are alienated from that collectively shared subjective notion of a community of others. In societies that alienate, the subject no longer feels any identity with the objects that he or she makes or the society in which he or she lives.

The power of capitalism does not stop at crude material domination. Through a myriad of means it shapes people's thoughts, ideas, desires and values. It controls their minds. It seeps into their language. It colours the quality of their relationships. People communicate as object to object, using each other, fighting each other in a dehumanized, materialistic world. So pervasive and subtle is this climate, men and women are not even conscious of how the economic system distorts their essential being. In the family and the school, in the workplace and the market, through the media and the law, a certain way of thinking about matters is conveyed. We accept the rightness, the normality, the appropriateness of so many features of ourselves and society. Such control of the consciousness, the very way we see ourselves and other people, is what is meant by 'ideological hegemony'. In the words of Marx and Engels (1965):

The ideas of the ruling class in every epoch are the ruling ideas: i.e. the class, which is the ruling *material* force in society, is at the same time its ruling *intellectual* force. The class, which has the means of material production at its disposal, has control at the same time over the means of mental production, so that thereby, generally speaking, the ideas of those who lack the means of mental production are subject to it (p.60).

Burrell and Morgan (1979) record their review of Gramsci thus:

The ruling class always seeks to legitimate its power through the creation and perpetuation of a belief system which stresses the need for order, authority and discipline, and consciously attempts to emasculate protest and revolutionary potential (p.289).

Under the trenchant eye of critical theorists, capitalism's long ideological reach is seen to grasp every cultural and social activity. Science, technology, education, welfare, language, family life, art, music and literature are all prey to its hold. Technological progress and efficiency, the logic of industrialization are the by-words for an advanced civilized society, but they reject the humanity of people and instead produce a 'one-dimensional man'. Technology is a political force. It wants people equipped, intellectually, psychologically and practically, to serve the needs of capital. An ostensibly content, materially replete people is anaesthetized from the true experience of being human.

All of this is recognized by radical psychologists who see their own discipline as largely the product of dominant capital interest. They believe that it is no accident that psychology has chosen to study people as objects. Trying to be like the natural sciences only dehumanizes people. Heather (1976, pp.41–2), for example, sees most traditional, positivist psychology being most interested in predicting and thereby controlling behaviour. However, he goes on to ask, to what ends is this control directed, who is to do the controlling and who is to be controlled? These are political questions. Both psychology and psychiatry have become part of capital's attempt to control people. They do this by defining what is normal, sane and acceptable, which rules out some people and their behaviour from taking part in everyday life. They try to 'mend' those who are failing as mothers, husbands, workers, schoolchildren and well-behaved citizens. They mask the true cause of many personal difficulties by blaming the individual and his psychopathologies and not the harsh, competitive and callous social system with which some people just cannot cope. In case the reader feels that the radical psychologist exaggerates her case, Heather quotes Eysenck as an example of how far the psychologist as natural scientist is prepared to go:

> The problem to be discussed is: how can we engineer a social consent which will make people behave in a socially adapted, law-abiding fashion, which will not lead to a breakdown of the intricately interwoven fabric of social life? . . . The psychologist would answer that what was clearly required was a technology of consent – that is, a generally applicable method of inculcating suitable habits of socialized conduct into the citizens (and especially the future citizens) (ibid., pp.46–7).

### Radical practice

For all brands of rádical humanism, the programme of action is the same. People should become aware of how social experience, particularly in a capitalist society, limits their thinking, shapes their outlook, dulls their senses and channels their desires. All social phenomena, whether religion or systems of justice, are the creation of human beings even though some come to dominate and oppress the human experience. Through the effort of 'self-consciousness', individuals can recover their own true being and so change the society in which they live. Lukacs, for example, saw the proletariat needing to achieve its class consciousness, needing to understand how capitalism profoundly influences and controls every aspect of the lives of its members, as a prelude to the revolutionary overthrow of capitalism. Similarly, radical psychologists help people find a personal liberation from social conditioning. They gain:

> A greater understanding of, and a greater degree of control over, *their own* behaviour and experience, *their own* relationships with others, and *their own* place in the social order (Heather 1976, p.60).

Others prefer to cast a critical eye on society's penetrating influence on language, technology and the general intellectual climate. Ultimately it is these which determine people's state of consciousness. It is not just a matter of understanding, and so implicitly accepting as the interactionists do, the construction of everyday life. There is a need to understand the pathology of such constructions.

The wish, then, is to express the true, extensive nature of capitalism, thereby raising people's consciousness about the penetrating power of society to shape beliefs, control values and create needs. Unlike the functionalists, who take the basic character of society for granted, the radical humanist challenges the very fabric and alleged self-evident virtue of society and its mechanisms. The style is less that of the political activist and revolutionary and more that of the intellectual critic. Technology and science, ideology and language all become part of the system of power and domination. This has to be recognized and exposed. It is the task of the critical theorist to help articulate this condition and raise the consciousness of people living within society. This points the way to alternative forms of living, social relations which are more humane and wholesome. In such a society, the individual would be poised to recover his or her own subjectivity and his or her freedom.

Freud held a pessimistic view of human nature. It needs restraining. Drives need to be repressed. Society's role is to control, check and regulate the potentially brutish side of the human make-up. In contrast the radical humanist is an optimist, at least as far as human potential is concerned. As we have seen, this is reflected in her view of the ideal society. Only when society caters for the needs of people and not the needs of capital will we see the flowering of the human spirit and the full potential of men and women.

The exotic combination of political critique and concern for the individual tempts many a social worker. There is a passionate quality underlying much of what goes on in this paradigm. The personal and the political are viewed as inextricable. However, in practice the starting point is the personal – the state of mind, the subjective outlook, the level of consciousness of the individual.

As we run through the structure of a radical humanist practice for social workers, we see that, although the overall aim is to change the social order, the route taken is via the client's understanding of his or her own situation. This is the platform from which radical change has to begin.

At almost every turning, the radical worker's practice is a mirror-image of that offered by the traditional, functionalist practitioner. Society is a problem for the individual; the individual is not to be seen as a problem for society. Clients are best able to explain their difficulties, not professional experts. Similarly, clients have the capacity to generate their own solutions. Expert-imposed answers are alien. They perpetuate the client's oppressed condition. It is with such thoughts in his mind that Illich *et al.* (1977) refer to doctors, teachers and social workers as the 'disabling professions'. Working with people collectively is much better than working with them individually. It is not surprising, therefore, that, when radical social workers speak, their fiercest words are for the traditional caseworkers and the state organizations that breed them.

The second half of this chapter considers the distinctive orientation that a radical perspective gives to each stage of the social work process. In this sequence we shall pay particular attention to one theoretical outlook which is assuming increasing importance. Conceived in the seventies, born in the eighties, feminist theory and practice is set to develop into a major social work perspective (for example, see Brook and Davis 1985; Dominelli and McLeod 1987; Hudson 1985). Most practising social workers are women. Most clients are women. These facts alone make the appearance of a feminist theory for practice an event of considerable significance.

## Defining the problem: the political cause of personal problems

Individuals who are confused by their situation, unfulfilled in their work, estranged within their family, at odds with the whole tenor of society and what it stands for have a problem. If it affects their behaviour and they become difficult and abusive or peculiar and disconcerting, other people will define them as a problem. Feelings of depression and purposelessness or pressures of expectation and obligation reduce social living to an empty experience.

Capitalist society defines people on the one hand as producers of capital through an exploitation of their labour. On the other, it treats them as consumers of the products of the capitalist economy. Their status is that of an object in the face of the needs of capital which is impersonal and inhuman. This is alienating. It is the nature of capital to treat people who labour not as human beings but as 'things', commodities to be shifted around whenever the demands of ever cheaper and efficient production require. As Jones (1983, p.66) reminds us, time and time again Marx wrote of the struggles of working class people to resist the dehumanizing tendencies of capitalism. It is important to the ideology of capitalism that the individual's experience is understood as self-made. It resists the notion that the economic system is to blame. Loneliness and depression. despair and the feeling that life is no more than a treadmill is seen as natural, it is simply the essence of the 'human condition'.

We can see all this at work in the way children are instrumentally schooled for their eventual use as productive, self-disciplined citizens. It is recognized in the workings of the judicial system which controls those who fail to live up to the required standards of a productively useful and well-behaved workforce. It can be detected in the remote manner in which health and welfare services are offered by self-proclaimed experts in matters of everyday living. People feel no identity with the social institutions that bear on their lives. Welfare bureaucracies do not belong to the people. This certainly includes the personal social services which are experienced as impersonal and intrusive as welfare officials judge behaviours and measure social standards. Clients are not involved in the design of services or their delivery. They are experienced as alien. They are imposed. Welfare systems satisfy the needs of the state and not the needs of the people served, the majority of whom are working class. Social services are disabling.

Women live in a man-made world. Their performance in this world can result in them being defined as a problem. In a society dominated by masculine values and opinions, ideas and standards, women will be asked to evaluate themselves by measures and concepts that are foreign to their way of being. Collins (1986) states:

> The feminist analysis for this 'sexual politic' . . . enables one to not only understand individual and collective female oppression but also what is seen as our cultural 'consciousness of estrangement'. Feminists believe that the primary emphasis on the instrumental masculine, whether individual or societal, invariably requires estrangement from the 'whole' of life, nature and being (p.215).

Women are defined in terms of their competence, or rather incompetence, as mothers and wives, and they are judged by their sexual behaviour. When women perform incompetently or unacceptably in these areas they are perceived to be a problem or to have a problem. However, the problem for women is that these are standards and measurements by which others have chosen to judge them and by which they are expected to judge themselves. Feminists are beginning to understand the extent and depth to which women are oppressed both materially and ideologically. This oppression denies them the opportunity to value the significance of their own experience of being a woman. Instead their experience is defined through a language that originates outside their own experience (Graham 1983, p.146). Thus:

> Many of the problems that women experience may be attributed to the social context rather than to internal inadequacies . . . 'failure to cope' might be reinterpreted as an understandable reaction to an unhealthy situation (Donnelly 1986, p.37).

### Explanation and assessment: analyzing personal troubles in a political context

Whenever one group has the power to define the situation of another, the effect on the members of the subordinate group can be assessed in terms of the climate of control set by the strong. The methods by which dominant groups determine behavioural expectations and standards have to be identified.

Just as important is the need to understand how such subjugation affects the individual's psychological as well as sociological state. Feelings of impotence, despair and a fatalistic acceptance of the hopelessness of one's condition describes the mood of many social work clients. The language we use, the families in which we live, the television we watch, the newspapers we read all help to shape our understanding of what is right and proper, what is normal and good:

> Concepts of normal and abnormal behaviour, health and illness, sexual roles and conduct, human needs, education, work, family

and community life are supplied by a range of institutions which act as 'vehicles of cognitive domination' (Whittington and Holland 1985, p.31).

For feminists, gender is a fundamental factor in the assessment of any situation that involves women. Whenever inequality is met, whenever we find one group which is dominant and another which is subordinate, we must be alert to the nature of this difference and understand how it is being maintained. McLeod (1986) states:

> We are all equal irrespective of our gender. Consequently social relations that obliterate this fact must be challenged and transformed into social relations that reflect and create equality in terms of gender (p.55).

An analysis of circumstances that involve women must take as its starting point the relationship between the personal situation and the social context in which it is set. The analysis must be sensitive to the state of mind of the individual woman and the social, political and ideological climate in which that state of mind occurs. There is a pervasive, insidious politics of everyday life that we hardly recognize, so total is its presence. However, it shapes our lives, it casts some as powerful and others as weak, it allows some to judge and requires others to be judged. This political fact of life has to be identified, analyzed and thoroughly understood before action which is to be appropriate and effective can be taken.

### Aims: become aware and take control

People need to recover control of their own minds. In so many subtle ways, individuals are encouraged to understand themselves, and therefore assess themselves in terms of society's dominant expectations. Those who do not meet these expectations must be, according to societal standards, abnormal in some way. Most of us accept these definitions of ourselves. Therefore, if we do not behave and feel in the ways we think that we should, we feel disturbed and dissatisfied, frustrated and confused, angry and depressed. In contrast to the radical structuralist, the radical humanist does believe that changing people is important. Galper (1973) says that:

> The oppression of our society is not only laid on us, it is in us and perpetuated by us . . . so we must work to change people's politics, consciousness, and personalities . . . We must affirm people as people and empathise with their pains and hopes at the same time that we challenge the parts of them that are limited and oppressive (p.43).

Equally important is the recognition that, like education, social work *is* politics, and necessarily means political activity. Davies (1982, p.180) introduces social workers to the work of Freire. Education, says Freire, should aim at fundamental change. And what is true for education, believes Davies, is true for social work. The goal of education and welfare is to 'politicize' learners and clients to the point where they can see the need and value of gaining power for themselves.

People have to become free, they need to reclaim their own subjectivities. The aim is to recognize how others define us to suit their interests. The production of critical awareness is known as 'consciousness raising'. It encourages an active responsibility for whatever psychological, sociological or political condition in which we find ourselves. People should not simply accept other people's descriptions of the way things should be. Women should not accept men's definitions. The handicapped should be wary of prescriptions meted out by the physically whole. This fight against society's ideological assumptions and the way they adversely define certain groups has been most marked in the case of women and black people. Less developed, but equally pertinent, is the need for such groups as old people and the handicapped to resist society's devaluation of them.

In broad terms, two clear aims characterize a radical practice. The first is to raise the consciousness and understanding of those groups who experience some form of subjugation. They must learn to recognize how others shape their experience of themselves. They must recover control over their own experiences and personal destiny.

The second aim is for groups to seek greater control over the services and resource made available to meet their condition. Rather than exist as passive recipients of expert practices, clients should become active producers as well as consumers of resources defined under their direction.

### Methods: consciousness raising and achieving control

In order to achieve the two aims, two *methods* are available: individuals taking hold of their own consciousness; and individuals also taking control of their own situation.

The first method involves the individuals finding ways to become aware of their condition and the situations that promote it:

> Critical consciousness (or conscientisation) is concerned then, with challenging the given categories of thought with which people order their social world and think about themselves. It addresses 'ways of seeing' in John Berger's phrase, and is eventually a strategy for cognitive renewal; an approach to reappropriating a consciousness which has been hijacked by systems of meaning which are alien to the individual's quest for an accurate grasp of their reality (Webb 1985, p.92).

'Consciousness raising' can be practised between a social worker and her client on a personal basis, but the more usual and potent method is to gather people similarly affected. As a group they are well placed to explore their experiences and their situation. They can begin to recognize how their own state of mind is linked to the values and demands of wider society. They can help each other gain in self-understanding through which comes a growing sense of personal responsibility, freedom and power.

The second method really flows from the implications of the first. Not only should individuals take a hold of their own consciousness, they should also take control of their own situation; they should seek to do something about the circumstances that conspire to determine their behaviour. This being the case, clients must become actively responsible for understanding their own needs, defining their own problems and determining their own answers. Consumers of health and social services all too often lay passive before the self-proclaimed expertise of doctors, teachers and social workers. Professionals peddle remedies that perpetuate the problem. The client is kept a passive object and not encouraged to be an active subject. Consumer self-awareness, understanding and responsibility challenge the official response. They also demonstrate the ability of people to determine their own destinies, create their own solutions and organize their own answers. Thus, in the style of Freire, clients and social workers alike should reflect on their condition, then act on it and in so doing transform it:

> Mutual aid and self-discovery are encouraged in this paradigm; professionalism and social distance between helper and helped are reduced to the minimum. Cooperative, non-hierarchical forms of work, problem-solving and domestic life are fostered. Social workers are encouraged to seek strengths from tackling issues collectively as feminists have done. One way is the development through grassroots unionisation of a power base to challenge social deprivation and oppressive public policies (Whittington and Holland 1985, pp.31–2).

## Feminist social work

A feminist social work practice has distinctive properties. The work of Donnelly (1986) illustrates them nicely. She writes about two women social workers, employed by the Social Services Department, who started work with a women's group in North Braunstone, a large, deprived, run-down council estate in Leicester. The women of the estate were no strangers to the attentions of social workers. Implicitly, and often explicitly, they were held responsible for the way their families behaved. This seemed unfair to the social workers, Stella and Alison, who described how they started:

We got to talking about the way that women are treated as clients — about how women are 'done to' rather than having any sort of power in their own lives and that social work actually perpetuates that and makes it worse. And we thought of ways that we could work to make that better — for them to have more control over their own destiny (ibid., p.18).

The group identified six aims for itself:

1 To combat isolation by enabling women to realise they are not alone in their difficulties and by building up friendship and support networks extending beyond the group situation.

2 Through group work to develop an awareness of women's oppression in society and how this affects them as individuals.

3 To build up self-confidence and self-esteem, enabling women to develop their own potential.

4 To enable women through the group process to realise the power they have and to begin to gain greater control over their lives.

5 To enable women to articulate their feelings in order for them to come to terms with painful experiences.

6 To increase self-awareness and help women to gain a better understanding of their bodies (ibid., p.19).

Working together in a group was recognized as a key method. It meant that problems were not experienced as individual failure but recognized as a common consequence of trying to deal with extremely difficult circumstances: private troubles are the result of social conditions. Individual women were not alone with their problems. Learning to recognize the underlying social origin of personal troubles was appreciated by all group members. Here is Cathy giving her account of the process:

We're talking about health problems that particularly affect women, which range not only from menstrual difficulties and childbirth and post-natal depression, but just general depression and anxiety, which more and more of us are realising now is a result of the situation we're in, you know, and that it's not a particular weakness in women but it's more to do with the situation women are in (ibid., p.24).

Throughout feminist social work there is an insistence that women learn to recover control over their own lives. This affects every aspect of practice. Many of social work's techniques perceive and assess women in terms and categories that have no bearing on *their* view of the situation and what *their* life means to *them*. The techniques merely serve the interests of Social Services Departments and match established views of what a well-managed service-delivery system should be doing with its clients. *But women should speak for themselves and social workers should learn how to listen.* Feminist methodology, says Rose (1982):

> Begins and constantly returns to the subjective shared experiences of oppression . . . within feminist theoretical production the living participating 'I' is seen as a dimension which must be included in an adequate analysis (p.368).

Hudson (1985), too, makes a strong case that feminist social work has to develop its understandings from the day-to-day experience of women clients and workers. Indeed, she argues that 'theorizing from the personal is a feminist principle from which social work can . . . learn' (ibid., p.636).

Women have to be encouraged 'to tell their story' and social workers have to listen if they are to understand and if they are ever to help these women understand. For Collins (1986, p.215), the feminist method is one of 'gleaning political insights from an analysis of personal experience'. The normal methods of social research and professional interviewing hear nothing of the real experience of women:

> As we have listened for centuries to the voices of men . . . so we have come more recently to notice not only the silence of women but the difficulty of hearing what they say when they speak . . . the failure to see the different reality of women's lives and to hear the differences in their voices stems in part from the mode of social experience and interpretation (Gilligan 1982, pp.173–4).

Groups in which women can tell their story and where they can share experiences, where they offer love, care and support represent an entirely different method of learning and understanding. Help comes from other women and not the detached expertise of professional workers.

Two things emerge from this experience. One is a sharpened awareness of the nature of the shared condition and its effect on each individual. This leads to greater self-understanding. The other follows in the wake of this 'raised consciousness'. To be aware and to understand is to begin the process of resuming control over one's life. The research by Brown and Harris (1978) shows that there was a link between clinical depression and the circumstances under which women lived. Individual women tend to see their depression as a result of their own deficiencies. Donnelly (1986, p.23) quotes the work of Weitz. She analyzed a consciousness-raising group and concluded that it helped women realize that blame was more appropriately attached to external conditions. This realization also helped them increase their sense of control which in turn raised their self-esteem and reduced depression. Having recovered self-control, the next step is to do something about those factors that determine one's daily experience, which is what the North Braunstone women did.

The group gave the women individual and collective strength – but what to do with it? Like many feminist groups before them who had established Women's Aid refuges, Rape Crisis Centres and well-women clinics, they took political and practical action. A major road scheme was scheduled to run through their estate. If built, it would ruin the quality of life for all those who lived there, but particularly the women at home all day with young children. A series of campaigns and public demonstrations found many of the women taking a very active part. Others battled to increase state benefits. A 'Reclaim the Night' demonstration spoke to the hearts of yet other group members. Nearer home, the group itself never neglected the fundamental task of fighting for better resources for the women and children on the estate. The last word is with Cathy, one of the North Braunstone women:

> It's magic really that it's the Women's group that are actually breaking through that sort of blanket depression on the estate . . . that they're actually standing up and saying, 'No, we don't have to take things lying down – we can fight them' (Donnelly 1986, p.41).

The radical perspective receives further illustration in the next chapter. It is set within the probation service. The work can be described as socialist welfare work or radical probation practice, but, however it is described, the orientation of the social work remains true to the principles of the radical humanists, those raisers of consciousness.

# 13 Radical Practice

## Radical practice in probation work

At first sight, a radical social work practice in the probation service looks distinctly unpromising. Probation officers are tied to the courts. They are deeply implicated in issues of law and order, so any overly critical questioning of the state and its attitudes towards criminals seems professionally precarious. Most probation officers practise in ways that reflect the state's assumptions that the service exists to correct the behaviour of criminals. They do this as individual, autonomous operators practising on individual, involuntary clients. This is not the stuff of radical practice. Nevertheless, in spite of this unpropitious background, there are a number of writers and practitioners who have begun to work out what a radical practice might look like. We shall briefly acknowledge a couple of them before moving on to consider the achievements of McLeod. She offers a practical example of working with prostitutes in the probation setting and her stance is that of the radical.

First and foremost, a socialist probation practice requires the officer to make a critical analysis of the state and the part the service plays in it. This understanding affects all aspects of the job: how clients are viewed and approached, how their problems are defined, how they are tackled. Fundamentally, 'this involves resisting the correctionalist perspective underpinning much probation work' (Walker and Beaumont 1981, p.175).

One of the most regular themes is that probation officers should learn to see their clients not as individuals pathologically predisposed to commit crime, but as just one example amongst many of how someone is trying to cope with the demands of living in a capitalist society. Casework's treatment of 'faulty personalities' is at best irrelevant and at worst ideologically suspect when applied to the working class clients of the probation service. The juridical system seeks the 'transformation' of the individual into an obedient citizen. Walker and Beaumont (ibid., p.147) note the probation service's emphasis on casework, the one-to-one relationship, and, 'above all, probation records, which are used to document the personal details of each individual and the measurement of progress towards normality over time'.

This analysis leads to a preference by radical workers for collective action: collective action by clients and collective action by officers.

Hugman (1980) rallies:

> The individual fighting a lone battle may be able to stimulate change, but his power is as nothing to the power of the group, area, district or union. There are few issues or problems round which a group of some kind cannot be formed, and many which cry out for the tapping of wide resources (pp.138–9).

There is persistent faith in the collective strength and resources of people to find their own solutions. The very act of bringing people together is politically significant. The individualization of crime, the belief that the malady lies in the mind of the criminal, masks other ways of understanding the 'deviant' act. Thus, the practical injunction is to bring people together, work in teams and join the union.

Walker and Beaumont give a good example of how such thinking influences practice. Here it is in full:

> It is proposed in your office that a group work approach should be adopted with unsupported mothers and their children. You are interested and go along to a planning session. You are horrified to hear the ideas that others have — teaching 'good mothering', homecraft and other useful womanly skills! However, you are able to point out to colleagues the values they are promoting and persuade them to focus the group more on the provision of a creche, self-help activities and some consciousness-raising discussion (Walker and Beaumont 1981, p.181).

The National Association of Probation Officers (NAPO) is an important outlet for the growing political consciousness of many probation officers. It matters that there are officers prepared to state publicly that prison is destructive, that there are unjust laws and that law enforcement is discriminatory. NAPO has become increasingly active in a variety of penal policy issues. It supports the decriminalization of soliciting, sus and other vagrancy offences, drunkenness offences and the possession of cannabis. It is opposed to the over-exhuberant use of imprisonment which is the knee-jerk response of successive right-wing governments.

We now have the flavour of radical probation practice. It is time to consider an example in more detail. Eileen McLeod, before moving into social work teaching, was a probation officer. Her work with prostitutes provides a splendid illustration of how changing your perspective shifts your practice.

### Probation officers and prostitutes

Prostitution is officially classified as a 'vice'. In itself it is not a crime. However, the related activities of soliciting and loitering are offences. It is with these that the prostitute is normally charged under the 1959 Street Offences Act.

The Wolfenden Committee, reporting on prostitution in 1957, was quite clear that, if women could be referred early on in their careers to the probation service, they might yet be reformed of their unfortunate habits. The Committee was equally clear that imprisonment was a necessary option for the courts dealing with prostitutes. Prison acted as a threat which would make offenders more willing to accept the help of the probation officer.

So what did probation officers do with prostitutes who were on probation? Were they successful in helping them mend their ways? Did other methods of working with these women suggest themselves? McLeod, in a series of papers and a book, asked and answered these questions (McLeod 1979, 1981, 1982). Her thinking and practice display many of the characteristics of the social worker as radical humanist.

Initially, McLeod analyzed the work of probation officers with a small sample of prostitutes on probation. In the main, the officers adopted a common approach. They explained the client's criminality in terms of her personality or particular circumstances. By and large the aim was to control the women's illegal behaviour, usually by trying to keep her activities within the law. Officers encouraged women to stop soliciting. They also tackled those problems whose solution they believed would lessen the pressure to solicit. For example, quotes McLeod from an officer's file (1979, p.460), 'Carol had a good work record up to a year ago and if this ability to work could be rediscovered it would prove a minor turning point'.

This way of thinking was in tune with prevailing ideas about what 'caused' women to become prostitutes. Glover (1969) saw women's entry into prostitution as evidence of a personality defect, a symptom of their psychopathology:

> The fact that a prostitute barters her body for filthy lucre is psychologically speaking neither so surprising nor so unnatural as it seems. It is . . . one more proof that prostitution is a primitive and regressive manifestation (p.15).

If this is the explanation, then treatment, reform and counselling are the order of the day. However, in pursuing such aims, the officers failed miserably. Within the first nine months of the probation order, reports McLeod (1979), of the twenty women:

> Ten had further convictions, nine for soliciting and one for brothel keeping. By the end of the year, another three had convictions for soliciting and one had a caution that would have been a conviction had she not given a false name (p.460).

The probation officers' work appeared firmly rooted in the soils of a scientific, diagnostic and treatment oriented practice. McLeod finds it striking that, without exception, probation officers defined problems in individual terms and aimed to tackle them on an individual basis:

> There were no references to the possibility of working with prostitutes in small groups, as women who might have various problems in common. Nor were structural factors discussed as possibly enhancing the attraction of involvement in soliciting or as making it difficult for women to disengage from it. No mention was made for example of the part that low pay for unskilled women might play, if they did want to work, or of the effect that the scarcity of child care facilities might have on the possibility of taking up ordinary work (ibid., p.459).

Thinking about the prostitute as someone who was a problem and had a problem meant that probation officers failed to address a major structural factor underpinning the women's behaviour: society's stark unequal allocation of power and resources. Dominelli (1986, p.87) also notes that social workers attempt to repress the deviant behaviour of the individual woman and replace it with non-deviant behaviour. This, she believes, demonstrates the validity of Liazos's point that in an unjust and exploitative society, no matter how 'humane' agents of social control are, their actions necessarily result in repression.

### Towards a radical practice

So, what should a radical probation officer do? McLeod practices as well as preaches a socialist line. Her outlook is that of a feminist. This meant that she was 'on her guard against tolerating adverse social conditions among women' (1981, p.63). She was against seeing prostitutes as necessarily suffering personal shortcomings. Rather, their involvement in prostitution seemed a reasonable choice in the face of difficult economic and social circumstances. Most of the women were young, unskilled single parents with few social or material resources to fall back on. The alternatives to prostitution were low paid, routine jobs which were difficult to combine with bringing up young children. This is how Dominelli (1986) sees it:

> So, it was not individual failings that pushed women into prostitution. Rather, prostitution was a rational response to the subordination and powerlessness which these working class women experienced as the sum total of their lives . . . By organising their own work schedule, prostitutes could compensate for society's failure to provide publicly funded, flexible child care provisions . . . By procuring and securing their own livelihood in adverse circumstances, prostitutes were able to assert some power in defining the shape of their own lives whilst being structurally placed in a relatively powerless position (p.81).

Prostitution as a psychopathological condition is fiercely rejected. Imprisonment is seen as harsh and ineffective, and if anything making matters worse, particularly if the prostitute is a mother with young children. Fines are laughable. If poverty encourages a woman to turn to prostitution in the first place, the only way to pay a fine is to do some overtime using the only skill that pays them reasonably well.

Working as a radical humanist, the practitioner will: appreciate how things look from the point of view of the women; help them not only define the problem, but advance solutions that suit them; work collectively; and seek changes in the cultural and legal climate that defines the behaviour of the women in such an adverse and unfair way. McLeod did all these things.

The more McLeod worked with the women, the more impressed she became with their personal strengths and abilities. This gave the lie to the patronising view (for example, the Howard League observations made in 1974) that prostitutes are inadequate people with low self-esteem. Established opinions were prone to argue that, since these women were incapable of helping themselves, they should be helped, that is treated and rehabilitated into a proper, moral way of life. The more McLeod talked with prostitutes, the more convinced she became of the injustice of their situation. Some were prepared to act. Along with a small number of local probation officers and lawyers she canvassed the idea of a group. Such a group could help understand the problem. It could look at ways to try and do something about their difficult legal and social circumstances.

**Collective action**

In 1975, a 'drop-in-centre' was set up in the local red light area. This produced discussions out of which many of the prostitutes felt that 'something should be done' about their situation. Talking about their work, it became clear to all that, relative to their poor employment opportunities in the conventional job market, prostitution offered better pay. The women could set their own pace and work hours that allowed them to fit their work around family commitments. However, the constant threat of arrest, fines and imprisonment was a worry. Moreover, the Street Offences Act was felt to be profoundly unjust. It takes two to solicit, but only the prostitute is subject to legal process and legal sanction. The man is ignored by the law. And if that is not unfair enough, in court proceedings, a woman who has had a previous conviction is entitled to be described by the court as a 'common prostitute'. This is read out as she is charged; that is *before* the case is heard. This clearly prejudices her chance of an unbiased hearing.

These were the problems. The explanation lay in the experiences of poverty and powerlessness of the women, social hypocrisy and the biased workings of the law. A year later, the group had evolved into a pressure group. It went under the acronym PROS (Programme for the Reform of the Laws on Soliciting). Its specific aims were:

1 To remove prison sentences for the offences of loitering and soliciting for the purposes of prostitution.
2 To abolish the term 'common prostitute' in legal proceedings.
3 Ultimately, to remove the offences of loitering and soliciting for the purposes of prostitution from the Statute book (McLeod 1981, p.61).

PROS ensures that the voice of the street prostitute is heard. It insists that she participates in any discussion about the issue of prostitution. However, it was felt to be more than just a self-help group. 'Consciousness-raising' became an important method, allowing members not only to understand their particular experience but also to help them recognize what could be done about their situation. Out of this developed the campaign to reform the law on street offences. Attention was deflected from individuals and on to the campaign. A permanent address and telephone number were secured. Allies offered protection. The issue was brought to the notice of the media. PROS made various appearances on television, radio and in the newspapers. The intention throughout was that the group would be 'client led'. It was therefore important that the prostitutes themselves articulated their position, spoke on behalf of PROS and appeared before the media. In this work, the women grew in confidence, became practised at public speaking and gained in self-respect. To describe these women as 'inadequate' or 'sick' was grossly inaccurate.

Solidarity was also sought with other organizations. 'Sisterhood' with the Women's Movement was obtained — in particular, a group of women within NAPO (the probation officers' union), collaborating with PROS:

Were successful in getting decriminalisation of offences relating to prostitution established as official NAPO policy and securing the affiliation of NAPO to PROS. This . . . enhanced the campaign's public standing, besides providing support and cover for probation officers around the country who want to organise in connection with it (ibid., p.73).

Further links were made with the upper-class call-girls' organization, the English Collective of Prostitutes, and together they lobbied Parliament to seek the decriminalization of prostitution.

## Organizing for power

Throughout the writings of radical social workers there is the insistence that personal troubles must be understood as public issues. The women's emphasis on consciousness-raising fused the personal and the political. Acting together develops alternative bases of power for both the women and the professionals. This helps counter the established perspective that views the women as psychologically weak and sick.

Dominelli, in discussing McLeod's work, recognizes that women, and in particular working class women, enjoy very little power. 'People's behaviour and activities,' she writes (1986, p.67), 'are political because they make statements about the power relations inherent in any given situation.' So, prostitution, for example, depicts the way in which power is derived from gender and is used by the more powerful gender to impose its definitions and prescriptions on the less powerful one. The only way to fight the imbalance is to unite. Dominelli talks approvingly of PROS. By creating a group with its own identity, prostitutes gained in collective strength and personal confidence. They learned to 'speak out and to do so in their own terms' (ibid., p.82).

It is by organizing that the powerless can overcome their powerlessness. However, at this point we are beginning to drift into the world of the radical structuralist.

# 14 The Revolutionaries

## Radical structuralism

For the radical structuralist, the social world, like the natural world, is a real and concrete place. Social events are regarded as determined, particularly by society's economic arrangements. Thus, a materialist view of the social world is offered.

However, whereas the empiricist believes that we know reality through our direct experience of it, that it has an independent, factual, external existence which we may discover through our senses, the structuralist offers a more indirect version of how we know this objective, material reality. For the structuralist there is, indeed, a material, objective world, but, to understand why it is like it is, the observer has to look to the underlying conditions or structures that give rise to it. These structures are not directly observable, but have to be appreciated through theoretical assertions. There is a rejection of the empiricist's passive orientation to the material world, that it is simply there to be discovered by those who have eyes to see and ears to listen. Rather, knowledge of the material world is gained through acting upon it, holding ideas about it, trying them out and seeing if they work. It is to these underlying material conditions that the structuralist has to turn in order to explain 'surface' phenomena such as social relations and psychological processes.

In particular, there is general interest in the social consequences of capitalism. Louis Althusser, for example, says in his interpretation of Marx that men and women do not make history. It is inclined to make them. So, says Wright Mills (1963):

> The economic basis of society determines its social structures as a whole as well as the psychology of the people within it ... The class struggle between owners and workers is a social, political, and psychological reflection of objective economic conflicts (pp.82–3).

Life, wrote Marx, is not determined by consciousness but consciousness by life (1977, p.164). It is in the way that people respond to their material needs that determines both their psychology and their society. It is the way that people come together, or are brought together, to make a living that allows us to say that economic relations produce social relations. It is the economic relation of one man or woman to another that colours all other relationships. Economic relationships certainly determine the political and ideological climate of a society. The first requirement of the radical structuralist, therefore, is to understand the ways in which the economic system influences all other aspects of life.

We need to understand how wealth is produced. In capitalist societies the means of production are in the hands of a small group. They hold the capital and are the ruling class. In order to create wealth and accumulate capital, the labour power of working class people is required. However, they receive, in the form of wages, only a portion of the value of their labour. The surplus value is retained or, more accurately, appropriated by the owners of capital and the means of production. They call this profit and it makes them rich. The labour power of the working classes is, in a word, exploited. This produces profoundly unequal economic relationships which are reflected in the social, political and ideological relationships between the ruling class and the working class.

Although the ruling class needs the labour of the working class, to the extent that the working class wants to keep a larger share of the surplus value, they pose a problem for the owners of capital. This sets up an inherent conflict of interests between these two major groups. As will be seen, the ruling class, using the apparatus of the state, seeks, in all kinds of ways, to keep the lid on working class aspirations and dissatisfactions. Perhaps, for social workers, one of the most important of these is to create a way of thinking that masks the true nature of working class difficulties. Essentially, the problems of the working classes are that they are poor, powerless and the victims of gross economic inequalities. The accepted wisdom, by rich and poor alike, is that we get what we deserve by our own efforts. It must be the case, according to bourgeois reasoning, that the condition of being working class or poor or failing to cope is of one's own making. Such difficulties are the result of limited abilities, which, 'naturally', are not rewarded. Naturally, too, talent should be rewarded. Those at the top are obviously there because of their abilities.

It is not the case that the ruling class overtly brow-beats the working class into submission (although this does happen). For most of the time, the subjugated condition of the working class is not recognized, and the unequal order of things is taken to be the natural order of things. The powerful do not have to display their power by crudely coercing the powerless. The whole business of maintaining social order is much more subtle. Lukes (1974), in his analysis of power, points out:

> The pluralists suppose that because power, as they conceptualise it, only shows up in cases of actual conflict, it follows that actual conflict is necessary to power, but this is to ignore the crucial point that the most effective and insidious use of power is to prevent such conflict existing in the first place (p.23).

One of the ways in which behaviour in a capitalist system can be understood is to house it in a psychological framework which encourages a view of the person as an abstract, highly individualized entity, the understanding of whom requires no necessary reference to the world in which they find themselves. The work of Leonard (1984, and with Corrigan 1978) on this topic is most important. It is of considerable relevance to social workers and is worth looking at in a bit more detail.

## Psychology under capitalism

The types of psychology that develop under capitalism will reflect the economic and social conditions of that system. There is a broad tendency to neglect the material conditions of the individual and place the emphasis on a psychological understanding solely inside the head of the individual. Capitalism sponsors a psychology that encourages a view of men and women as personally responsible, as psychologically discrete and isolated individuals who are products of their own internal psychological goings-on. People are as they are because of how they are personally made. Human beings have an essential quality that will express itself irrespective of the material circumstances in which they happen to find themselves. These qualities transcend time and place, culture and society. People's emotions and ideas cause their behaviour, for which they are personally responsible. The context in which such emotions and ideas come about is ignored. It would be highly dangerous to suggest that the personal inadequacies of the poor, the deviant and the difficult were the product of their downtrodden economic and social experience.

Psychoanalytic theory, suggest Corrigan and Leonard (1978, pp.115 –16), develops by the use of introspection. Inevitably the emphasis is on the subjective experience as the basis for explaining psychological problems. There is less heed paid to the social nature of human beings and their consciousness. Behaviourists offer an even more narrow psychology. They have a crude, mechanical view of human behaviour in which the individual passively responds to the world around. The effect is all one way. It misses the much more complicated manner in which individuals relate and inter-relate with their physical and social environment. People are affected by and affect what is happening about them. All phenomena, continue Corrigan and Leonard must be seen as the product of material existence. The individual's consciousness is also a product of this material reality:

> This is not, of course, to argue that consciousness does not in its own effect material reality, but the overall determination lies with material existence. But to understand the dialectical relationship between human consciousness and material existence is different from the idealist conception which dominates much

of psychology in the West, which somehow separates mental processes from material reality . . . It follows . . . that there is no place in a Marxist approach to individual existence and personality for any conception of basic human nature. What is *human* is a social product and a result of the interaction between man and the social world; man becomes man as a result of this interaction (ibid., p.119).

## Conflict

Unlike the functionalist, the radical structuralist sees society as a changing entity, evolving not through co-operative endeavour, but through conflicts cf interest, power and resources. The constant realignment of individual and group interests leads to shifts in the social structure. Whereas major disturbances are seen as pathological by the functionalists, here they are seen as endemic and to be encouraged. Groups pursuing their own interests are the motive force behind societal change. There is a perpetual tension between the have and the have-nots; those with the power and those without; those enjoying the goods of society and those not; those who dominate and those who are dominated. Such contradictions lead to increasing tension in social structures. The eventual result is a crisis – political as well as economic – which produces a new economic and social order. In contrast to the radical humanist, the radical structuralist is less concerned with improving the individual's state of consciousness and more intent on changing the structural patterns of society by fighting for a new economic order and a redistribution of power.

Much of the work of Marx and Weber triggers the thinking that takes place within this paradigm. Burrell and Morgan (1979, p.349) record that both men saw capitalism representing a new mode of social organization, certainly different from and in some ways better than feudalism, but nevertheless beset by its own forms of repression, oppression and human bondage. Weber, for instance, considered the unequal distribution of power and authority in society as a major force behind the seething quality of social life.

Sociologists such as Dahrendorf and Rex have picked up these insights. Conflict is a characteristic of social living. People group around common interests but these interests will conflict with those of others. Relations between groups, therefore, are defined at first solely in terms of the conflict situation. For example, the residents of Acacia Avenue do not want, as they see it, insane, sex-crazed psychopaths as neighbours at number 43. However, this is not how a psychiatric self-help group views things. Its members believe that the quiet, leafy suburbs found around Acacia Avenue offer the ideal environment for the rehabilitation and recovery of people who have experienced a difficult and fragile psychological time. Paraphrasing Rex, in most cases the conflict situation will be marked by an unequal balance of power so that one group emerges as dominant and will seek, with all the resources it can muster, to impose its preferred view of the situation.

For conflict theorists, the most important task is to analyze society in terms of structures of power and authority. Society is seen as 'factionally' divided rather than functionally coherent. Whereas the followers of Marx concentrate on the deterministic effects of the economic base of society, radical Weberians see the dominating forces in society's 'superstructure' where the conflict of interests between different power groups are most evident:

> Thus there is often a primary concern for the role of the state and the political, legal, administrative and ideological apparatus through which dominant interest groups secure their position within society (Burrell and Morgan 1979, p.356).

This last quote gives a clue to where some radical social workers pitch their efforts. If they are not aiming to overthrow capitalism through bloody revolution, which for most social workers feels overly ambitious, then there is work to be done in opposing the established interests of dominant groups. Such interests are expressed in the form and distribution of resources, values and ideas:

> An understanding of who does the defining, of what is defined as a social problem and how it is defined, as well as who shapes legislation and in which ways, is clearly crucial to the student of the welfare state (George and Wilding 1976, p.2).

The probation service, for example, deals mainly with working class clients. This, it is argued, is the result of laws which identify certain forms of activity as illegal, activities that are more likely to be committed by working class men and women. It has also been argued that the characteristics of social work practice are determined by the characteristics of welfare law and policy. 'As the characteristics of the law vary between client groups, so varies the character of social work practice between client groups' (Howe 1986b, p.140).

Practically, the social worker seeks to expose and challenge the political base that underpins legislation. Radical workers place clients at the receiving end of capitalist class-biased social sanctions. This position requires welfare workers to understand the relationship between clients and the state. Laws and policies are not neutral. They are politically inspired. The state and its machinery serve the interests of the dominant class. If social work is to be about promoting the well-being of subordinate classes, then the state's machinery has to be examined critically. In order to change and improve the practice of social work, it is necessary to alter welfare law and policy at both central and local government level. Social Services Departments are the sum of the structures that 'concretize' prevailing political ideologies. These determine the nature and identification of problems whether amongst the old, or children and their families. Thus:

> Structures are actually *constructed* not as the simple intentions of individuals but through political struggle. It follows from this that political struggle can deconstruct and reconstruct the structures within which we practise (Bolger *et al.* 1981, p.99).

As will be seen, Marxist social work demands that practice is explicitly political.

In practice, it proves difficult for social workers to act in ways that are always consistent with the requirements of this paradigm. Welfare work itself is analyzed as part of the state apparatus. It is designed to mop up the adverse consequences of capitalism, maintain an obeisant population and ensure a healthy, educated labour force. To the extent that social workers are successful in softening the worst effects of gross material inequalities and anaesthetizing the population to the real origins of their problems, they are bolstering capitalism. In part, the development of the welfare state is the price capitalism is prepared to pay for political stability. By keeping the lid on dissatisfaction and unrest, social workers are one of many state-sponsored occupations that help stifle the inherent conflicts of a capitalist society. Thus they delay the eruption of crisis and the ultimate downfall of capitalism.

### Defining the problem: problem people and people with problems under capitalism

Those without power and resources are liable to suffer in a capitalist economy. Materialistic societies view people as objects, as commodities. They are expected to move home and community to follow the needs of capital as industry shifts from one part of the country to another. Their labours help create a surplus value which is appropriated by the owners of the means of production. Those who cannot and never will provide labour (the old and the mentally handicapped), those who will not provide labour (the feckless, the deviant and the ill-disciplined) and those who live in the wrong place (areas of high unemployment) are of no use to capital. Therefore they pose a problem. They will also suffer problems because they will lose out heavily in the fight for resources. Bad housing, low income and poor prospects characterize the lives of the unemployed and the unemployable. Jones (1983) argues that it is poverty and its consequences which are the cause of so many people becoming the clients of the personal social services. The overwhelming majority of clients are not wage earners.

Spitzer (1975) makes similar distinctions. There are those who are of no use to society, whose labour is exhausted such as the old. They are treated as 'social junk'. They have no social value. And there are those who are a threat to society. They are disruptive and antagonistic. This group includes the unruly and delinquent, the mentally unstable and the ideologically unsound. Spitzer calls these people 'social dynamite'. They have to be controlled. The state is prepared to spend much more on the disruptive than on the useless. Law and order issues attract more state attention and resources than those who need care and compassion. Thus, according to this analysis, people become clients in one of two ways. There are those who, like the old, are economically dependent; and there are those who, like the criminal and violent, are economically threatening. While the functionalist talks of care and cure, the Marxist hears control and contain.

Under the cold smile of caring capitalism, the behaviour and circumstances of the working classes, whatever their ages, are kept in check. The relationship between the state, social workers and the working class is determined by the problems the working class pose for capital. There is a specific problem, 'namely how to control the working class and especially its poorest elements and so ensure that the balance of class forces remains safely in the interests of capital' (Leonard in Jones 1983, p.xiv).

This way of approaching the delinquent and disruptive, the old and the handicapped is calculated to remove them from the political agenda. To designate them as sick or deranged denies them social currency. In turn, this:

> Reinforces the view that the solutions to problems of clients are to be sought in the efforts of welfare professionals rather than in fundamental and radical social change. As a result, one of the running sores of capitalism is politically sanitised, and clients — rather than becoming a source of outrage and a stimulus to militancy on account of their suffering and neglect — become at best objects of pity or at worst stigmatised outcasts who have only themselves to blame (ibid., p.64).

So, to anticipate one of the methods of a socialist practice, social workers should expose capital's brutalization of working class men and women.

### Explanation and assessment: a structural analysis

In the broadest sense, explanations of social problems have to be understood in terms of the consequences of a capitalist mode of production. The state is a mechanism for one class maintaining control over another. In our society, the state serves the long-term interests of the ruling class and the needs of capital. The inequities inherent in capitalist modes of production are bound to produce people who are without some basic resource. This may be money, opportunity, good schooling, adequate housing, a job or a sense of purpose. This will mean that some basic need is not being met.

Situations can be understood only in terms of who holds the power and who does not, whose interests are being served by this policy or that practice and who is losing out. The social worker needs to keep asking, 'how much control do these people have over matters which are affecting their lives?' Questions also have to be asked about why, for example, spending has increased on the provision of tranquillisers for young, fraught mothers but has decreased on the provision of day nurseries. Or why the number of supplementary benefit investigators is growing but not the number of tax inspectors for top income earners.

It must always be understood, too, that the problems of the working class are economically determined. The socialist welfare worker resists the idea that an individual's problem behaviour is simply the result of some inner psychological malfunctioning which can be put right by a spot of personal treatment. The problems of the working class are defined by the demands of the ruling class. It is in their interests to diagnose social and behavioural difficulties in individual, psychological terms and not in economic and political ones. Each 'case' is seen as an instance of individual failure. The following is an example of how the radical structuralist explains some aspects of child-care policy and practice.

Jones (1983, pp.13–16) plots the formation and development of child-care services since the turn of the century. Essentially such services concern themselves with the quantity and quality of the country's future labour reserves: the number of children needed, their health and fitness, their attitudes and standards of behaviour. A favourite theme of policy formulators is the worry about the large number of children who appear 'spoiled' for the labour market by their family background and upbringing.

By the 1950s, the 'problem family' had been identified. These families constituted a huge drain on welfare resources as far as governments were concerned. They produced more than the average number of children, many of whom never developed the right attitudes to work and were lost to the labour market, being more inclined to follow a life of crime and indolence rather than pursue an honest career. In times of growing affluence and opportunity, the only explanation of why these families failed had to lie with the families themselves. There was no other possible way to explain their inability to take advantage of the mounting prosperity that characterized the times except as some form of family mental sickness. Clearly, something had to be done about this chronic 'waste of human assets'. Either such children had to be rescued and rehabilitated or their families had to be treated. Accordingly, organizations such as the Family Service Unit and the local authority Children's Departments set about understanding the internal dynamics of these problem families:

They were to be seen as inadequate and immature, and although, later, the impact of adverse economic conditions upon them could not be completely denied, these remain in the background, and the individual defects of family members remained a prominent part of social-work diagnosis and social-welfare response (Corrigan and Leonard 1978, p.101).

The state continues its growing interest in the welfare of children. Its ability and willingness to sanction intervention into family life has increased. The basis on which it justifies such intrusions is always the same, 'the interests of the child', with never a hint that another answer might be 'in the interests of a well-ordered capitalist economy'.

Recently, the issue of child abuse has undergone such a series of definitions. 'Battered babies' were 'discovered' in the 1960s. The 'syndrome' was diagnosed initially in medical terms. The pathology — for such it clearly was — lay with the parents and it was they who were to be treated. Analyzing matters within a materialistic framework, Parton (1985) provides us with an elegant account in *The Politics of Child Abuse*. He describes how the disease model of non-accidental injury developed. He critically examines how its assumptions influenced policy, practice and research. Inexorably, the major professions built up the case that the problem lay in the character of the parents and their families. Child abuse work became a top priority for social workers. The response of social workers to individual cases received ever-closer scrutiny. Woe-betide any worker who failed to rescue or successfully treat a child who subsequently fell victim to the 'sick' behaviour of an abusing parent.

There is, however, a different way to think about child abuse (see Parton 1985; and in the States, Nelson 1984). Rather than see the problem residing with the malfunctioning of abusing parents or even the oddities of the child itself, Parton, for example, relates child abuse to class, inequality and poverty. Most abused children are from the poor working class. The stresses experienced by those who live in bad housing, on low incomes, in a state of insecurity and isolation can be intolerable. Blaming the family shifts attention away from the root causes of such behaviour — the profound inequalities present in capitalist economies. So long as child abuse is seen as a product of sick individuals, children will continue to be abused. Short-term answers lie in such things as a vast increase in nursery provision. The only long-term solution, though, is a radical change in the distribution of economic and political power.

Closer to home, social workers also have to understand the political nature of their own departments. The way social work is organized and resourced is a strong determinant of how social workers perceive, assess and practise their work (Howe 1986a). Expectations of what is appropriate practice are built into an agency's policy and procedures.

This allows Corrigan and Leonard (1978, p.102) to claim that 'in the welfare state and its services, ideology is embedded in the practice of social workers and the organisation and delivery of services'. In no sense can social work practice be politically neutral. Welfare bureaucracies steer social workers into seeing people and their problems in particular ways. Assumptions are made about the nature of clients and their difficulties. Methods, such as casework, imply an individualized pattern of pathology and treatment.

In their practice, social workers ask how to do it but not why. Techniques overshadow aims. Methods become purposes. In the 'technologicalization' of social work we hear of caseload management and priority scaling. Practitioners are on the look-out to do family therapy or run groups in order to exercise their favourite skills. Such assumptions, such definitions of how things are, can be challenged. Socialist welfare workers are obliged to examine their own organizations if they want to understand that which frustrates a radical practice and that which would help it to flourish.

For Jones (1983) the underlying analysis is not in doubt:

> The relationship of clients to the labour market is highly significant in both defining an individual's client status and as one of the determining forces shaping the styles and methods of social work (p.28).

If the state individualizes problems and produces 'cases', then social workers confirm this view by practising 'casework', treating pathologies and helping individuals to recover their proper social functioning within the capitalist system:

> Whether they are described as 'abnormal', 'inadequate', 'disturbed', or 'immature', clients are presented as 'peculiar' human beings, whose peculiarity is the reason for their inability to live and function as 'normal'. From this standpoint it is then possible to explain the material squalor and deprivations which characterise the circumstances of so many clients. Social work has never attempted to deny outright the material nature of client's problems, but rather locates it as a *symptom* of inadequacy ... It is in part the manner in which social work has figured as a theory and practice of idealism − namely, the primacy accorded to personality in the determination of an individual's social condition − that permits it to be accused of depoliticising the problems of clients. It is not simply that a materialist stance has been neglected but that it has been rejected and fought against (ibid., p.60).

Look through the opposite end of the telescope and you view matters as a radical structuralist. The capitalist economic system causes individuals their problems. Material conditions determine people's psychological experiences. Jones, as a fully committed determinist, rebukes social workers who see the mind as more dominant than matter in informing the human condition. Practice has to tackle the economic base and the ideological structures it supports if there is to be a real, lasting, socialist answer to the problems of the working class poor.

## Aims: the redistribution of wealth and power

On the minor as well as the major scale, the social worker aims to redress the balance in favour of the poor at the expense of the rich. A fairer distribution of resources and opportunities is demanded. Personal distress is relieved by more money and better housing, less pressure and improved communities. Socialists are committed to building a society in which there are fair shares for all: from each according to his ability, to each according to his need. Solidarity of interests is sought amongst clients and state employees alike. Social workers should resist demands made of them to act as crude agents of control, keeping in check the unproductive and the awkward. Probation practice, for example, should *not* be about changing attitudes, or adopting a correctional approach to deviance or transforming the individual into an obedient citizen. Rather, it should be about identifying the under-lying conditions that generate poverty and crime, and it should be about helping the powerless to claim more power. The cold, calculating and impersonal nature of both policy and practice in state welfare capitalism is exposed and criticized for what it is at every opportunity.

The intention, then, is clear: to improve the lot of the downtrodden. There is strength in acting in concert. There are ideological victories to be won in unmasking the self-seeking interests of ruling class practices. Nevertheless, the fundamental goal is never in doubt. 'In brief,' believe George and Wilding (1976, p.105), 'the welfare state cannot solve the social problems of today without the abolition of the capitalist system.'

## Methods: socialist welfare work

There are three ways for social workers to help clients improve the amount of power they possess and the resources they can secure. The first insists on helping clients fight every inch of the way to gain rights, entitlements and a fair share of whatever goods are around. Those with the greatest needs experience the poorest provision in our society. Welfare rights work is fundamental to good practice.

The second method requires a more polemical stance. At every opportunity, social workers should be arguing that social problems result from the harsh and inevitable consequences of a capitalist economy and the ideological climate set by the ruling classes. People who live in rotten houses, who subsist on meagre incomes and who have few opportunities to escape the bottom of the social pile are not well placed to behave 'reasonably'. Yet any signs of 'unreasonable' behaviour on their part is liable to be severely checked and punished. The law frowns on those who try to earn extra money by prostituting themselves, doing odd jobs while on supplementary benefit or keeping the eldest daughter at home and away from school to look after the baby while mum goes out on a part-time job. The socialist welfare worker must not collude with the state-guided response of 'blaming the victim'. The proper reaction is 'a deep and seething anger against a society which created such problems in the first place' (Jones 1983, p.74). Conflict is ever present in society, but it should not be resolved to maintain the *status quo*. Social workers should strive to promote it and use it to favour the working class.

The third element in the methodological style of the radical structuralist social worker is collective action. There is strength in numbers. Members of a group can support each other. Collectively, people are better able to analyze how the social structure determines their material and psychological life. By uniting in thought and deed, clients and social workers offer a more powerful political force in the face of significant issues. Social workers are advised actively to participate in trade union matters. Marxists recognize that the real power of the working class to bring about fundamental change lies in the workplace. Both the client and the social worker have to be linked to the local and national trade union movement. Together they can raise community issues and defend services.

Another power base for welfare workers is that of the team. The team is very important for the conduct of a radical practice. It not only offers a stronger power base, but also reflects the need to understand and respond with clients on a collective basis. Individualizing a client's problem receives a boost by allocating responsibility for its treatment to an individual 'case' worker. A team, particularly one which is non-hierarchical, is much better able to make a public issue out of a series of private sorrows. There is the collective ability to recognize common threads linking individual cases. A team approach also implies a community-sensitive style of practice. The socialist welfare worker, then, is intent on generating an organizational structure in which power is devolved to front-line team workers and clients. Decentralized departments are the preferred form of organization. Further, teams should meet up with client groups. Together, they should identify what clients feel to be their needs and determine how they should be met.

Clients, too, should be brought together, particularly where they have problems in common. Not only can each client learn to articulate his own situation and so recognize himself as the product of structural inequalities, he can also work out ways with others to fight a world which is intent on keeping him down and out. Whereas the state can comfortably handle discrete, personal client problems by seeing them as examples of individual pathology, it has greater difficulty in coping with groups of people who refuse to be seen as inadequate and who seek a better deal from society. Within capitalism, client problems are de-politicized and identified as a personal inadequacy. The casework method is always in danger of playing into the hands of a system which blames the individual and not itself. The Marxist social worker must ensure that *personal problems are seen as political issues*. It is incumbent on the social worker not to change the individual to fit the system but to change the system to suit the needs of the individual.

# 15 Marxist Social Work

Consideration will now be given to what a Marxist practice looks like in work with old people. There are two very good reasons for choosing this group. Firstly, many of the problems of old age are seen as the direct product of growing old in a capitalist society. Secondly, the elderly are a low priority, unfashionable area of practice for most professionals, precisely because old age and what it means are fashioned in the harsh value climate of capitalist economies. All the more reason then for taking an unflinching look at welfare work with old people.

## New outlooks on old age

Old people, particularly very old people, are one of the largest groups in the workload of social services teams. Their numbers are growing. Nearly 10 million people in the UK are aged over sixty. The increase in the population of the very old is having a major impact on the health and social services, made all the worse by cutbacks in the national welfare budget.

A ruse adopted by governments is to champion the notion of community care. It sounds wholesome, it has that rosy ring of nostalgia and yet it is an illusion. It is certainly meant to be cheaper, at least as far as its conservative proponents are concerned. In practice community care means family care – and family care means care by women, the ageing daughters of very old parents. 'Community care under these terms is a cheap option,' believes Phillipson (1982, p.49), 'but one which is in many cases rooted in stress and in moral blackmail of the most insidious type.' Lack of support in the community and the expectation that women should care unquestioningly for elderly relatives leads to stress, unhappiness and in extreme cases 'old age abuse': the attack on demanding old people by desperate, exhausted sons and daughters.

The elderly have never been a high priority in welfare provision. This has been reflected in the attitude and practices of social workers. Children and their families have always been more popular amongst professionals. In fact, social work with old people, on the whole, has been depressingly uninspired. Nor have researchers and academics helped. Exciting ideas are associated with work attached to families, children, young deviants, criminals and the mentally disturbed. All of which poses something of a problem for the radical social worker faced with the prospect of working with old people. As Phillipson (ibid., p.107) puts it, 'for those seeking radical therapies or political change, involvement with older people was judged to constitute a form of professional or political suicide'. In a series of brave bids to stay alive, Phillipson has written a number of excellent analyses and polemics in which he fashions a socialist theory and practice for work with old people. He develops a critical account of the position of elderly people in a capitalist society. This is his guiding principle: 'old age is less a biological and psychological problem, more a problem for a society characterised by major inequalities in the distribution of power, income and property' (ibid., p.1).

## The problems of old age

The first distinction to make is that between old people viewed as a problem and the problems that old people experience. The two are closely linked, for the consequences of finding old people politically to be a problem in its turn brings about many of the difficulties that the elderly themselves have in achieving a successful old age.

For governments, the main disadvantage of old people is that they consume but do not produce. They are rated as passengers, not crew (Ensor quoted by Jones 1983, p.25). For the politics of the right, the public sector represents a burden on the economy. If this is the formula, the elderly are one of the biggest burdens of all. Bornat *et al.* (1985, p.11) observe that old people are pinpointed as a major cause in the fiscal crisis, threatening government plans to lift the economy out of recession. The authors go on to quote one of Margaret Thatcher's speeches, given in 1984, to illustrate this way of thinking about old people:

> There will be a substantial increase in the number of old people relying on pensions and welfare benefits in the coming years, as well as an increase in the number of young people seeking further education. The working population now [have] to consider how much of their income must be allocated to this kind of expenditure (ibid., pp.11–12).

Indeed, the struggle to reduce costs is a major theme in the policy for the elderly. It has affected the quality of residential care, the level of domiciliary support and the adequacy of pensions. Such policies and provisions cause old people many problems.

Growing old affects the body, and for some the mind, in such a way that the physical and social environment also needs to change if a consistent life style is to be maintained. The ideal layout of a house alters with the age of the occupant. More money needs to be spent on fuel to keep warm, particularly if the individual is home all day. The problems of heating are made even worse when it is remembered that old people are more likely to live in poorly maintained, ageing property. The siting of shops, the provision of public transport, the number of chiropodists — all these become matters of considerable importance with increasing age. A deficit in any one or more of these areas presents an old person with major problems. Nationally, they add up to a huge social issue.

It is estimated that around 2 million people live at or below the poverty line. Most of these are retired working class. Phillipson (1982, p.10) notes that the lower an individual's income, the larger the percentage which has to be spent on basic necessities. It is hardly surprising, therefore, that the elderly poor suffer bad housing, inadequate heating and insufficient food. These cause stress. The combined effects of poor diet, cold conditions and too much stress produce a state of poor health which is greatest among the retired working classes. Some 700,000 old people are at risk of hypothermia. The 1981 Census records 163,250 houses in which a pensioner was living to be lacking both a bath and an inside toilet.

Norman (1980) examines the difficulties of the elderly from a different angle, but paints an equally gloomy picture. Using notions of freedom of choice, she sees that for those who are frail or disabled and living on a pension, what they might like to do and what physically and financially they can do, are all too often two entirely different things. The forms of treatment and care imposed on old people reflect what other people think is good for them but which may not be appropriate, helpful or necessary:

> Old people are taken from their homes when domiciliary support and physical treatment might enable them to stay there; they are subjected in long-stay hospitals and homes to regimes which deprive them of many basic human dignities; and they are often not properly consulted about the care or treatment to which they are subjected (ibid., p.7).

The important question to ask, therefore, is what can be done to safeguard the liberty of elderly people. It is no good leaving answers to the forces of the market. Old people will go under at every turn. The open market is a source of insecurity at a time of life when stability and consistency are important. Bornat *et al.* (1985, pp.54–5) mention the rise of private residential care in this context. Where there are profits there will also be bankruptcies. What is small and homely today will succumb to the advantages of economies of scale tomorrow. Rationalization of groups of small homes into larger, more cost-effective chains is already with us. On this line of analysis, the problems of old people are more accurately described as the problems that old people experience in a capitalist system. In contrast, the socialist welfare worker assesses matters as follows.

Consistent with the strictures of radical structuralism, the problems experienced by old people are determined by society's material conditions. A capitalist economy causes problems for elderly people. At best it is misleading to analyze an individual's difficulties in terms of their personal strengths and weaknesses. At worst, it deflects attention away from the real culprit – capitalism in all its cunning guises.

**Being old in a capitalist society**
The concern, then, is less with studying the characteristics of old age than with understanding how capitalist economies regard the elderly. In fact, put in its most radical form, the assertion is that social systems actually produce the characteristics of old age. Hence the title of Phillipson's book, *Capitalism and the Construction of Old Age*. The material and economic position of old people determines their social standing and the way in which they, and others, view being old. Through the mould of state policies, being old is fashioned and defined. Attitudes are set. Assumptions are made. The old learn what they are and what they mean. The lives of old people:

> Are inseparable from a web of economic relationships and it is these relationships which must be considered primary in influencing both the way in which we think about the process of growing old and the position of older people within the social structure (Phillipson 1982, p.154).

Any useful understanding of the problems of old age must accept this analysis: that the logic of capitalism as a productive and social system is irreconcilable with meeting the needs of elderly people. Capitalist priorities, whenever possible, relegate social and individual needs behind the search for profit and the demand for social stability, law and order which provide a suitable environment that help serve the interests of capital.

Throughout the lives of most people, great stress and value is placed on work and what is produced. For most people, work, and therefore production, stop somewhere between the ages of sixty and sixty-five. This, according to Corrigan and Leonard (1978, p.58), severs a vital link in the way people relate to society and experience their role within it. It is the essence of capitalist economies to:

> Stand in the way of the majority as individuals, because one of the most basic traits is to transform labour-power into a commodity and to pay it *at its value*, in other words according to the *minimal* conditions of its production and reproduction; in this respect, well before biological senescence indirectly comes into play, capitalist relations exercise an unceasing retarding influence (Seve 1978, p.362).

So we come to the main feature of being old in a capitalist society: old people do not produce or contribute to the economy but they do continue to consume. Their labour power has been exhausted. They are a drain on resources. Tinker (1981, p.5), in an otherwise most useful reference work on the elderly, is wrong to say that old people are not a deviant group, that they are ordinary people who just happen to have reached a particular age. In fact they do pose capitalism a problem. Other highly dependent groups, such as children, are treated differently by capitalism. They do consume, but they have the potential to become producers. Their labour power is in the future. It is therefore worthwhile investing considerable sums in the young and their families. In contrast, old people have no present or future economic value. They are a burden. This is how the Royal Commission on Population saw the elderly in 1949:

> The burden of maintaining the old does not consist in the money paid out as Old Age Pensions. It consists in the excess of the consumption by the old over their production. It is the fact that . . . the old consume without producing which differentiates them from the active population and makes of them a factor reducing the average standard of living of the community.

All of this conspires to define what old age means to society and the elderly themselves. They are, and therefore feel, useless, without value or prospect or purpose. Old age is perceived to be a time of dependence. There is an emphasis in policy and professional practice on passivity. Old people should expect less from life, and be grateful for what they do receive.

Again and again, we can spot how low is the value placed on old people and their needs. In the eyes of social workers, doctors and nurses they are the least preferred area of social work. They receive proportionately less attention by GPs and community nurses. There is discrimination in resource provision. For example, in 1980, whereas £33 per patient per day was spent on nursing in maternity hospitals, this figure drops to only £14 in geriatric hospitals (Bornat *et al*. 1985, p.43). Legislation for old people is negligible compared to that available for children, and what there is seeks merely to contain and sustain them in some basic state. The 1948 National Assistance Act is largely concerned with the provision of residential accommodation. Even so, governments tend to resolve the nuisance of dependency by transferring the burden of care and support from the state to the family (Jones 1983, p.26). More particularly, assert Corrigan and Leonard (1978, p.58), the bourgeoisie has tried to ensure that the working class should look after its own old age, through imposed insurance contribution and family care. The whole policy attitude towards the elderly, according to Parker (1965) is no more than a continuation of the Poor Law tradition:

The concern to maintain and foster family life evident in the Children's Act was completely lacking in the National Assistance Act. The latter made no attempt to provide any sort of substitute family life for old people who could no longer be supported by their own relatives. Institutionalised provision was accepted without question (p.100).

The logic of all this leads us to expect that the working class experience the greatest problems in their old age. Indeed, this is the case. The retired working classes are much poorer than the retired middle classes. They see retirement as an event imposed from the outside. 'Other people determine *when* you leave work, *how* you leave work and *how much* money you have to live on' (Bornat *et al*. 1985, p.18). Social work with the elderly, as with most other forms of social work, is overwhelmingly concerned with working class people. If we fail to appreciate this, adds Phillipson (1982, p.111), a major dimension of growing old is lost. To be working class, for young and old alike, is to receive less and suffer more throughout life. The result of all this is that if you are in social class V, you are two-and-a-half times more likely to die before you retire than if you are in social class I.

## Revolutionary aims
So, what is to be done? What are the aims of a socialist welfare practice? The analysis, which sees the very existence of social work as yet another state ploy to keep the problem of old people in check, tends to dampen the enthusiasm of the radical. However, as we have learned, although philosophers provide interpretations of the world, the point is to change it. This is what the socialist welfare worker seeks to do. To repeat the conclusion of the last chapter, social workers should not aim to change the individual to fit the system, they should aim to change the system to suit the needs of the individual. So extensive are the needs of old people that a system of individual referrals and personal treatments or tinkerings with the present array of resources is totally inadequate. A more radical approach is required.

In their *A Manifesto for Old Age* (1985), Bornat *et al*. announce a number of policy and practice proposals aimed at transforming the economic and social position of old people. We can identify three broad goals in the practice of the socialist worker: to educate old people about their condition, to seek political change through collective action, and to revalue the elderly. A little more can be said about each of these.

Firstly, social workers should aim to 'de-condition' old people about their own alleged limitations. 'People enter retirement', says Phillipson (1982, p 113), 'expecting to slow down, expecting their health to deteriorate fairly rapidly, and worst of all they enter retirement expecting "nothing".' Social workers should help old people rid themselves of the belief that they are a burden, that they should expect no more and be grateful for what they have. In fact, they should demand more. They certainly need it. They should fight those policies that deny them their rights and freedoms. Equality of treatment, whether social, economic or political, is a right. Old people have to reconstruct the experience of old age so that it is less damaging, less demeaning, and altogether more fulfilling:

> Transforming class and gender images of ageing and retirement must now be a major item on the socialist agenda. We need to construct a socialist policy which provides alternatives to the present system of retirement; to discuss egalitarian policies on pensions; to find policies for care which oppress neither the carer nor those who receive care. Above all, we need more liberating concepts to describe the experience of ageing (Bornat *et al.* 1985, p.19).

Secondly, social workers should help the elderly organize. This achieves two things: it brings people together in collective action; and it encourages the elderly to assume responsibility for their own campaigns. Identifying collective solutions to common problems is a prerequisite for appropriate practical, political action. For example, the London branch of the British Pensioners' Trade Union Action Association is demanding a single person's pension of 50 per cent of gross male average earnings in industry. Such organizations are often built around specific issues, particularly as they affect the retired working class. Links with the trade union movement are sought. A good example is provided by the Tooting Action for Pensioners, whose aims are:

> (a) to act as voice for the pensioners in Tooting; (b) to work with others to effect improvements in facilities for pensioners in the area; (c) to build up community links and identity with the area as a whole; (d) to campaign for workshops and occupation for retired people; (e) to fight for improvements in the state retirement pension (Phillipson 1982, pp.144–5).

Thirdly, and implicit in all action, is to challenge social attitudes. This affects old people at every level. It colours social policy, it influences the type and quantity of resources, it determines the way people work with the elderly. Each of these practices contains assumptions about what being old 'means'. It is from such actions that society, as well as the elderly themselves, learn to define old age. By challenging the prevailing structural and economic boundaries of old age, the elderly may learn to experience themselves positively and anew. For example, it should affect the day-to-day character of an old people's home. Norman (1980, pp.38–49) considers the rights and freedoms that people should retain when in residential 'care'. Old people should hold on to the freedom to control their own lives. This freedom should cover spending their own money, taking their own decisions and doing what they want so long as it does not interfere with the freedom of others. She quotes in full East Sussex's 'Residents' Rights' charter. This opens with the following sentence: 'what you have a right to expect if you live in one of the County Council's homes for the elderly'. It goes on to cover a large number of matters, including the right to get up and go to bed when you choose, the right to personal privacy, and the right to take the reasonable risks that a normal full life entails.

Socialist policies and practice aim to make growing old a natural part of the life-cycle, not a 'problem'. Phillipson (1982) approaches the end of his book by quoting Deacon on the ways in which radical policies will affect social relations. This is what old age would be like in a new age:

> The relationships between users and providers, producers and consumers, helpers and helped, administrators and receivers, would be transformed beyond recognition. The relationships would not be bureaucratic, not that of professional to client, not sexist or racist. Additionally it can be concluded that social policy would dominate economic policy and social policy would become a matter of realisation of human potential, the possibility of this potential being realisable because men and women would no longer be dominated by commodity fetishism (ibid., p.111).

### A Marxist practice

What are the methods by which such aims are to be achieved? Two principles guide practice: joint action, to increase the power of the otherwise politically weak; and direct involvement in planning and receiving a service by those who receive that service.

Marxist practitioners are most critical of social workers who individualize the problems of the elderly. Phillipson is particularly rude about those who advocate casework methods and therapeutic techniques. Here is caseworker Brearley's (1975) description of the basic social work task:

> [It] is the establishment of a relationship with the elderly client and the client's relatives or others in the immediate social net-work. As far as the elderly person himself is concerned the social worker can help him consider the realities of his current situation and discuss the available alternatives in the present. Beyond this it will be important to help him see an ongoing pattern in his life. Contentment in the present will depend on an acceptance that what has gone before has been relevant; in part it may also

depend on seeing value in the future. In this context reminiscence may have a therapeutic value in itself (p.109).

This is Phillipson's (1982) radical retort:

> To find meaning and satisfaction with one's past life is doubtless important. But can it be regarded as having equal priority with the current struggle of many elderly people for a decent income and adequate housing and heating? Such struggles are barely mentioned in recent social work studies on the elderly. These texts transform problems of class and gender into private experiences. Events which occur in ageing and retirement are identified as exclusively individual dilemmas, to be resolved primarily by individual casework . . . This perspective, I would argue, has led traditional social work theorising on the elderly into a blind alley, with the neglect of some distinctive features of social work practice with the elderly (p.110).

Collective action, then, is certainly one of the things to be done — but not in a politically neutral way. It is good that such organizations as Help the Aged and Age Concern campaign over such issues as low income and poor housing. It is bad that they do not frame them within a strong political and economic line. If the problems of old age result from the structural consequences of particular economic systems encouraged by certain political doctrines, then the problems of old age can be resolved only through political action. Social workers should become involved at local and national levels. They should help set up neighbourhood groups where old people can express their views, state their needs and determine responses. They should unite with residential staff, residents and their relatives to seek more resources. They should encourage a greater equality of power between old people as clients and welfare professionals as 'experts' so that, for example, residents can decide on such things as the time they have breakfast or whether they need help taking a bath.

So, doing it together and doing it for yourselves are important. They discourage tendencies towards deference and feelings of impotence. Stott (1981), in her spirited address, *Ageing for Beginners*, is certainly not to be found guilty of slipping meekly into old age. She sets out to reclaim the experiences of being old from the experts and the politicians and return them to where they belong, with old people themselves:

> People need politics — the art/science/methodology of getting things done by and for a community. The politics of catering for the 9,000,000 of us in the United Kingdom who are now pensioners are fascinating. Thousands upon thousands of people, paid professionals and goodhearted volunteers, are engaged in the job of helping to run our own lives — or that is what it seems like.

They sit together in committees . . . to decide policies for what we, the sixty-plus people, need and want . . . Isn't it as well that we who are conscious of ageing should take a sharp look at what they are, those bodies whose stated aim is to further and protect our interest, at who runs them, at which policies they endorse and campaign for? (ibid., pp.136–7).

I do not know whether or not he has read Stott, but the last word is with Mick McGahey (18 June 1986), a lifelong communist and vice-president of the National Union of Mineworkers. This is what he said about his own imminent retirement: 'communists don't retire. They change their position. I will join the pensioners and create hell among the pensioners.'

# 16 Theories for Social Work and Theories of Social Work

This book began with a reminder of what clients say about social workers. A strong theme in their reports was a preference for social workers who appeared clear about what they were doing and why they were doing it, and social workers who could say where they were going and how they were going to get there. Such clear thinking appears only when thoughts are explicitly arranged around a guiding theory. However, there is a second tier to the argument.

I have also sought to make the case that theory inescapably underpins practice and that different theories lead to different practices. In particular, different theories make different assumptions about two fundamentally important matters: the nature of man and woman and the nature of their society. The assumptions made about each one forms part of the basic character of that theory and its practice.

Even when a social worker claims not to be using theory in her practice, in fact she is still seeing people and their situations in one way rather than another. Perceptions can never be 'theory-free'. If we quiz her untethered thoughts, we soon learn that she is making significant and fundamental assumptions about her clients and their behaviour, about what makes them do the things which they do, about the way she comes to understand them, and about the kind of society in which they live. To deny this is to deny that the social worker is making any sense of the situation. If she is making sense of it, what particular sense is it which she makes? Making sense is a theory-saturated activity. Just because you cannot imagine how else to view matters does not mean that you are not holding a theory. It just means that your one theory is your entire world of sense. This is why I take issue with those who appeal to commonsense or declare themselves to be pragmatists or sit back in satisfaction and comfortably announce that they are eclectics.

## On commonsense, pragmatism and eclectic practices
If the appeal is to commonsense, we must ask 'sense' common to whom? Is your sense the same as mine? Do we have a sense in common? As has been seen, assumptions held about people and their situations may be at considerable variance. There is no obvious, self-evident way to view matters. Commonsense tends to mean the particular view held by an individual who cannot credit that there is any other way to see things. Or that the power of the ideological

climate over the ideas and assumptions held by most people is such that, indeed, they *do* see things in common and know of no other way of making sense. Bourgeois ideology is the ruling ideology. It has been around so long that it appears as the natural way of understanding society and its people (McLellan 1986, p.25).

This last explanation gives our first glimpse of a third tier: theories, particularly prevailing theories (which may become the commonsense), do not just pop up out of the blue. They are themselves the product of a deeper state of affairs. Theories about people and their situations reflect the dense web of ideas, beliefs and knowledge that characterize particular societies at particular times. This is why for much of the time most of us 'understand' our world, talk about it and approach it in ways that we hold in common. Ideas that are discontinuous with this experience would, if we followed them, wrench us out of our mental world. Such ruptures in our experience would be disconcerting. Most of us avoid them by denying that such new mental sets are possible. Embedded in our taken-for-granted world, radical views do not appear to make 'sense' or 'ring true'.

The pragmatist appears to proceed in a different manner. She says, 'if it works, do it' and 'do what can be done'. Again this avoids the issue. It ducks questions such as 'works for whom?', 'works to what purpose?' and 'works in what ways?'; and 'what can be done' might not be the same thing as 'what should be done'.

Pragmatists often claim to be realists, too. Quite what this means is not entirely clear, though it does sound something like:

> I know what is what. It is all very well having fancy ideas, but when it comes down to it the real world works in this way, no other, and if you are to get on with things, then you have to be realistic.

We are back with the problems met with having commonsense. Whose reality are we talking about? Being realistic tends to mean doing what is possible, but what is possible may in turn be determined by the assumptions held about people, their society and the political context in which thoughts and actions occur. Being realistic means sticking with your preferred reality, though your reality may not be mine.

The eclectic is the most slippery. She claims to take the best bits from different theories. They are chosen as those bits that most suit her purpose. The purpose is alleged to provide the resulting amalgam with unity and coherence. This may be true, for the individual social worker's purpose is unlikely to vary wildly from one piece of work to another such that she aims to cure clients of their emotional immaturity one day and then helps them gain greater control over the services of welfare departments the next. In practice the eclectic worker chooses bits from those theories that share a common outlook on the nature of men, women and society. The theories raided by the eclectic are usually sited within the same paradigm. There is an illusion of free movement through matters epistemological, ontological and methodological. In practice the eclectic worker holds a consistent view of people and their situation which restricts the theories which she uses in her construction of an eclectic practice.

## Two kinds of social work theory

My criticisms of those who appeal to commonsense, those who want to be pragmatists and those who feel comfortable as eclectics exist at two levels. The first has been conducted explicitly throughout the whole book: that all social work practices are unavoidably theoretical in so far as we all try to make sense of the world around us. The second has hardly surfaced, though it has lurked beneath all our discussions. It is this. Not only are our thoughts and actions theoretically informed, our theories themselves say something about the kind of activity we see social work to be. In social work, there are, then, two kinds of theory:

1    There are theories *for* social work. These are the ones that we have been trying to identify and understand in this book. They help explain people and their situations. They inform practice.
2    There are theories *of* social work. These seek to say something about the nature, purpose and character of social work itself. What is it about? What is its nature? What are its purposes? Who is it for? What should it look like when it is practised?

Now it may already have become apparent that a theory *for* social work also seems to imply a theory *of* social work. In other words, the choice of a theory *for* practice is also a choice about the kind of activity social work is taken to be. Further, just as different theories lead to distinct practices, so different theories also entail various notions of social work itself. With only a little reworking, theories *for* social work can be turned into theories *of* social work.

Although social work as a whole may be able to encompass different theories for various practices, it cannot also be true that, if a theory *for* social work implies a theory *of* social work, the activity as a whole can logically contain a range of theories of practice. If this were the case, it would suggest that social work can be about entirely different things, depending on the theory held. To allow such a range of theories for social work is to allow the idea that social work can be several contradictory things at once. Nor is it simply the argument that some theories might be better than others. It is being said that different theories in different paradigms declare social work to be a different activity.

Does all this mean that the social worker simply pays her money and makes her choice, that theories fight it out until one emerges as the winner? Well, that is one way to look at it. However, we can return to the earlier observation that theories *of* social work, and therefore theories *for* social work, emerge as products of their time and place. This helps us notice two factors about the current state of social work theory. The first is that by far and away the majority of social work theories are located in and around the 'functionalist' paradigm – the 'fixers' as I called them. The second factor is that, nevertheless, there are a considerable and growing number of theories that lie outside, and in some cases, well outside the functionalist frame of reference. So how do we make sense of this abundance of theory in, apparently, the one activity, social work?

### Consensus theories

The functionalists themselves expect that most theories will be in sympathy with their assumptions about people and society. After all, as far as they are concerned, this is how people and society actually do work and so theories that reflect this are bound to be appropriate, realistic and effective. Therefore they will be turned to and used most often. Such theories and their application help oil the wheels, keep things in order, and fix the parts which are broken. They help maintain society.

An outsider, though, offers a different explanation for these same activities. She accounts for the prevalence of 'mainstream', consensus theories precisely because, in maintaining order, they support society's vested interests. They offer ways of controlling people. At root, most social work theories preserve, in their thinking and practice, the *status quo*, that is, the interests of the dominant and established groups. The prevalence, success and apparent efficacy of traditional theories *for* social work merely indicates that they are compatible with the dominant theories *of* social work. Such theories work only in terms of the standards and assumptions contained in the dominant paradigm.

### Ferment and vigour in the state of social work

Nevertheless these reactions do not explain the sheer diversity of social work theory. Today they exist in a state of ferment. Historically we have witnessed a huge growth in the number and range of theories recommended for use by social workers. Elsewhere (Howe 1980) I have said that this might be taken as a sign of vigour and good health that one activity can sponsor such a range of intellectual fervour. Taking Kuhn's (1970) observations on the major changes that have occurred in the natural sciences, we too might note:

> The proliferation of competing articulations, the willingness to try anything, the expression of explicit discontent, the recourse to philosophy and to debate over fundamentals, all are symptoms of transition from normal to revolutionary research (p.91).

These suggestions hold some truth but already there are some new bids to make further sense of even these deeper structural thoughts. We may consider the work of Johnson *et al*. (1984) as an example of where we might yet take our thinking about social work theory and practice (also see Rojek (1986) who has already taken an early canter along this road). Johnson *et al*. see different theories working out their basic characters in relation to one another. The inherent complexity and tension in any social field will result in different viewpoints emerging. As participants argue and debate the attractions of seeing social reality one way rather than another, various theoretical positions develop. Rojek (1986, p.71) quotes Barthes who, in similar mood, invites us to consider statements of theory and practice not as 'a line of words releasing a single "theological" meaning but a multi-dimensional space in which a variety of [meanings], none of them original, blend and clash'. On this basis theories will have elements in common as well as elements in opposition.

It might also be the case that the proliferation of theory in social work indicates changes at a deeper structural level. As relationships (political and moral, economic and technological) between the individual and society become more complex, multi-faceted and contentious, so the theoretical expressions of these relationships become more varied. Each theory seeks to capture a key feature of social reality. The relatively simple relationship between the client and the social worker, the citizen and the state, which once was served by a limited number of basically similar theories, has now become much more fluid. The turbulent nature of the social substructure generates a wide range of social work theory, as practitioners attempt to make sense of the whole, dense spread of relationships, some of which 'blend' and some of which 'clash'. By its very nature, in its very position between the state and the individual, social work is bound to be buffeted by the full force of the tides and the tensions that comprise any social reality. There are no simple models of social work any more.

**Conclusion**

These are exciting thoughts. Longer term answers await further developments in the application of post-structuralist thinking to welfare practices. Meanwhile we have made substantial preparations, both conceptual and taxonomic. Those who wish to explore the heavens, first must build telescopes and chart the stars. It is necessary to plot rivers and map mountains long before the enquiring mind can sensibly ask why such features are there (rather than somewhere else) or why they exist at all. *We* have been mapping social work theories. We have been finding out where they are. We have looked at what they do; and we have seen where they lead us. Good practice requires social workers to know where they are and where they are going. Quite simply, there is nothing better than a clearly held theory to give the worker a good idea of place and a strong sense of direction.

# Bibliography

Adams, R. (1985), 'Truth and Love in Intermediate Treatment', *British Journal of Social Work*, vol.15, no.4, pp.391–400.

Allen, R. (1986), 'Custody — more to lose than liberty', *Community Care*, 1 May.

Argyris, C. and Schon, D.A. (1974), *Theory in Practice: Increasing Professional Effectiveness*, San Francisco: Jossey-Bass.

Atkinson, J.M. (1971), 'Societal Reactions to Suicide' in S. Cohen (ed.), *Images of Deviance*, Harmondsworth: Penguin.

Atkinson, J.M. (1978), *Discovering Suicide*, London: Macmillan.

Bailey, R. and Lee, P. (eds) (1982), *Theory and Practice in Social Work*, Oxford: Blackwell.

Ball, C. (1981), 'The Use and Significance of School Reports in Juvenile Court Criminal Proceedings: A Research Note', *British Journal of Social Work*, vol.11, no.4.

Bandura, A. (1977), *Social Learning Theory*, Englewood Cliffs, New Jersey: Prentice-Hall.

Bannister, D. (1966), 'Psychology as an Exercise in Paradox', *Bulletin of the Psychological Society*, 19, pp.21–26.

Becker, H.S. (1963), *Outsiders: Studies in the Sociology of Deviance*, New York: Free Press.

Biestek, F. (1961), *The Casework Relationship*, London: Allen and Unwin.

Bolger, S., Corrigan, P., Docking, J. and Frost, N. (1981), *Towards Socialist Welfare Work*, London: Macmillan.

Bornat, J., Phillipson, C. and Ward, S. (1985), *A Manifesto for Old Age*, London: Pluto Press.

Bottoms, A.E. and McWilliams, W. (1979), 'A Non-Treatment Paradigm for Probation Practice', *British Journal of Social Work*, vol.9, no.2, pp.159–202.

Brake, M. and Bailey, R. (eds) (1980), *Radical Social Work and Practice*, London: Edward Arnold.

Brandon, D. (1979), 'Zen Practice in Social Work' in D. Brandon and B. Jordan (eds) (1979).

Brandon, D. and Jordan, B. (eds) (1979), *Creative Social Work*, Oxford: Blackwell.

Brearley, P. (1975), *Social Work, Ageing and Society*, London: Routledge and Kegan Paul.

Brenner, C. (1955), *An Elementary Textbook of Psychoanalysis*, New York: International Universities Press.

Brewer, C. and Lait, J. (1980), *Can Social Work Survive?*, London: Temple Smith.

Briar, S. (1966), 'Family Services' in H.S. Maas (ed.), *Five Field of Social Service: Reviews of Research*, New York: N.A.S.W.

Briar, S. and Miller, H. (1971), *Problems and Issues in Social Casework*, New York: Columbia University Press.

Brook, E. and Davis, A. (1985), *Women, The Family and Social Work*, London: Tavistock.

Brown, G.W. and Harris, T. (1978), *Social Origins of Depression*, London: Tavistock.

Burrell, G. and Morgan, G. (1979), *Sociological Paradigms and Organisational Analysis*, London: Heinemann.

Butrym, Z. (1976), *The Nature of Social Work*, London: Macmillan.

Butrym, Z. (1981), 'The Role of Feeling', *Social Work Today*, 17 November, pp.8–10.

Cashmore, E.E. and Mullan, B. (1983), *Approaching Social Theory*, London: Heinemann.

Clare, A.W. (1981), *Let's Talk About Me: A Critical Examination of the New Psychotherapies*, London: British Broadcasting Corporation.

Cohen, P. (1968), *Modern Social Theory*, London: Heinemann.

Collins, B.G. (1986), 'Defining Feminist Social Work', *Social Work*, May–June.

Corby, B. (1982), 'Theory and Practice in Long Term Social Work', *British Journal of Social Work*, vol.12, no.6.

Corrigan, P. (1979), *Schooling the Smash Street Kids*, London: Macmillan.

Corrigan, P. and Leonard, P. (1978), *Social Work Practice Under Capitalism: A Marxist Approach*, London: Macmillan.

Craib, I. (1984), *Modern Social Theory*, Brighton: Wheatsheaf.

Cupitt, D. (1985), *The Sea of Faith*, London: British Broadcasting Corporation.

Dare, C. (1981), 'Psychoanalytic Theories and the Personality' in F. Fransella (ed.) (1981), *Personality*, London: Methuen.

Davies, B. (1982), 'Towards a Personalist Framework for Radical Social Work Education' in R. Bailey and P. Lee (1982), *Theory and Practice in Social Work*, Oxford: Blackwell.

Davies, M. (1977), *Support Systems in Social Work*, London: Routledge and Kegan Paul.

Davies, M. (1985), *The Essential Social Worker: A Guide to Positive Practice* (2nd edn), Aldershot: Gower.

Denzin, N.K. (1970), *The Research Act in Sociology*, London: Butterworths.

Dominelli, L. (1986), 'The Power of the Powerless: Prostitution and the Reinforcement of Submissive Femininity', *Sociological Review*, 34 1.

Dominelli, L. and McLeod, E. (1987), *For Welfare: Creating Feminist Social Work*, London: Macmillan.

Donnelly, A. (1986), *Feminist Social Work with a Women's Group*, Social Work Monograph no.41, Norwich: University of East Anglia.

England, H. (1986), *Social Work as Art: Making Sense for Good Practice*, London: Allen and Unwin.

Evans, R. (1976), 'Some Implications of an Integrated Model for Social Work Theory and Practice', *British Journal of Social Work*, vol.6, no.2.

Ferard, M.L. and Hunnybun, N.K. (1962), *The Caseworker's Use of Relationships*, London: Tavistock.

Fischer, J. (1978), *Effective Casework Practice*, New York: McGraw-Hill.

Fonagy, P. and Higgitt, A. (1984), *Personality Theory and Clinical Practice*, London: Methuen.

Freud, A. (1936), *The Ego and the Mechanisms of Defence*, London: Hogarth Press.

Galper, J. (1973), 'Personal Politics and Psychoanalysis', *Social Policy*, no.4 (November–December).

George, V. and Wilding, P. (1976), *Ideology and Social Welfare*, London: Routledge and Kegan Paul.

Gilligan, C. (1982), *In a Different Voice: Psychological Theory and Women's Development*, Cambridge, Mass.: Harvard University Press.

Glover, E. (1969), *The Psychopathology of Prostitution*, London: The Institute for the Study and the Treatment of Delinquency.

Goldstein, H. (1973), *Social Work Practice: A Unitary Approach*, Columbia: University of South Carolina Press.

Goldstein, H. (ed.) (1984), *Creative Change: A Cognitive-Humanistic Approach to Social Work Practice*, New York: Tavistock.

Goldstein, H. (1986), 'Toward the Integration of Theory and Practice: A Humanistic Approach', *Social Work*, September–October.

Graham, H. (1983), 'Do Her Answers Fit His Questions? Women and the Survey Method' in E. Garmarnikow *et al.* (1983), *The Public and the Private*, London: Heinemann.

Halfpenny, P. (1979), 'The Analysis of Qualitative Data', *Sociological Review*, vol.27, no.4, pp.799–825.

Hall, C.S. and Lindzey, G. (1957), *Theories of Personality*, London: Chapman and Hall.

Haralambos, M. (1985), *Sociology: Themes and Perspectives*, Slough: University Tutorial Press.

Hardiker, P. and Barker, M. (1981), *Theories of Practice in Social Work*, London: Academic Press.

Hearn, J. (1982), 'The Problem(s) of Theory and Practice in Social Work and Social Work Education', *Issues in Social Work Education*, vol.2, no.2.

Heather, N. (1976), *Radical Perspectives in Psychology*, London: Methuen.

Herbert, M. (1978), *Conduct Disorders of Childhood and Adolescence*, Chichester: John Wiley.

Herbert, M. (1981), *Behavioural Treatment of Problem Children: A Practice Manual*, London: Academic Press.

Hollis, F. (1964), *Casework: A Psychosocial Therapy*, New York: Random House Press.

Hollis, M. (1977), *Models of Man*, Cambridge: Cambridge University Press.

Howard League for Penal Reform (1974), *Comments on the Home Office Paper on Vagrancy and Street Offences*, London.

Howe, D. (1980), 'Inflated States and Empty Theories in Social Work', *British Journal of Social Work*, vol.10, no.3, pp.317–40.

Howe, D. (1986a), *Social Workers and their Practice in Welfare Bureaucracies*, Aldershot: Gower.

Howe, D. (1986b), 'Welfare Law and the Welfare Principle in Social Work Practice', *Journal of Social Welfare Law*, May, pp.130–43.

Hudson, A. (1985), 'Feminism and Social Work: Resistance or Dialogue?', *British Journal of Social Work*, vol.15, no.6, pp.635–55.

Hudson, B.L. and Macdonald, G.M. (1986), *Behavioural Social Work: An Introduction*, London: Macmillan.

Hugman, B. (1980), 'Radical Practice in Probation' in M. Brake and R. Bailey (eds) (1980).

Humphrey, N. (1986), *The Inner Eye*, London: Faber and Faber.

Hutten, J. (1972), 'Psychodynamic Approach to Casework', *Social Work Today*, 24 February, vol.2, no.22, pp.5–10.

Illich, I. *et al.* (1977), *Disabling Professionals*, London: Marian Boyars.

Johnson, T. *et al.* (1984), *The Structure of Theory*, London: Macmillan.

Jones, C. (1983), *State Social Work and the Working Class*, London: Macmillan.

Jordan, B. (1979), *Helping in Social Work*, London: Routledge and Kegan Paul.

Kaufman, W. (ed.) (1957), *Existentialism from Dostoevsky to Sartre*, London: Thames and Hudson.

Kuhn, T. (1970), *The Structure of Scientific Revolutions*, Chicago: Chicago University Press.

Leonard, P. (1975), 'Explanation and Education in Social Work', *British Journal of Social Work*, vol.5, no.3.

Leonard, P. (1982), editor's Introduction in C. Jones (1983).

Leonard, P. (1984), *Personality and Ideology: Towards a Materialist Understanding of the Individual*, London: Macmillan.

Lukes, S. (1974), *Power: A Radical Analysis*, London: Macmillan.

McCall, G. and Simmons, J. (1966), *Identities and Interactions*, New York: Free Press.

McLellan, D. (1986), *Ideology*, Milton Keynes: Open University Press.

McLeod, E. (1979), 'Working with Prostitutes: Probation Officers' Aims and Strategies', *British Journal of Social Work*, vol.9, no.4.

McLeod, E. (1981), 'Man-Made Laws for Men? The Street Prostitutes' Campaign Against Control' in B. Hutter and G. Williams (eds), *Controlling Women*, London: Croom Helm.

McLeod, E. (1982), *Women Working: Prostitution Now*, London: Croom Helm.

McLeod, E. (1986), 'You in Your Small Corner: A Discussion of "Feminist Social Work with a Women's Group"', *Issues in Social Work Education*, vol.6, no.1.

Macaulay, T.B. (1889), *The Miscellaneous Writings of Lord Macaulay*, London: Longmans Green.

Marx, K. (1977), *Selected Writing* (ed. D. McLellan), Oxford: Oxford University Press.

Marx, K. and Engels, F. (1965), *The German Ideology*, London: Lawrence and Wishart.

Mattinson, J. and Sinclair, I. (1979), *Mate and Stalemate*, Oxford: Blackwell.

Mayer, J. and Timms, N. (1970), *The Client Speaks*, London: Routledge and Kegan Paul.

Meyer, C. (1976), *Social Work Practice* (2nd edn), New York: Free Press.

Nelson, B.J. (1984), *Making an Issue of Child Abuse*, Chicago: University of Chicago Press.

Norman, A.J. (1980), *Rights and Risk: A Discussion Document on Civil Liberty in Old Age*, London: N.C.C.O.P.

Parker, J. (1965), *Local Health and Welfare Services*, London: Allen and Unwin.

Parton, N. (1985), *The Politics of Child Abuse*, London: Macmillan.

Peck, D. and Whitlow, D. (1975), *Approaches to Personality Theory*, London: Methuen.

Perlman, H. (1957), *Casework, A Problem-Solving Approach*, Chicago: University of Chicago Press.

Phillipson, C. (1982), *Capitalism and the Construction of Old Age*, London: Macmillan.

Pincus, A. and Minahan, A. (1973), *Social Work Practice: Model and Method*, Itasca, Ill.: Peacock.

Pointing, J. (ed.) (1986), *Alternatives to Custody*, Oxford: Blackwell.

Rees, S. (1978), *Social Work Face to Face*, London: Edward Arnold.

Reid, W. and Epstein, L. (1972), *Task-Centred Casework*, New York: Columbia University Press.

Reiner, B.S. and Kaufman, I. (1959), *Character Disorders in Parents of Delinquents*, New York: Family Service Association of America.

Roberts, R.W. and Nee, R.H. (eds) (1970), *Theories of Social Casework*, Chicago: University of Chicago Press.

Robinson, M. (1978), *Schools and Social Work*, London: Routledge and Kegan Paul.

Roche, M. (1973), *Phenomenology, Language and the Social Sciences*, London: Routledge and Kegan Paul.

Rojek, C. (1986), 'The "Subject" in Social Work', *British Journal of Social Work*, vol.16, no.1.

Rose, H. (1982), 'Making Science Feminist' in E. Whitelegge *et al.* (1982), *The Changing Experience of Women*, Oxford: Martin Robertson.

Rutter, M. (1975), *Helping Troubled Children*, Harmondsworth: Penguin.

Sainsbury, E. (1975), *Social Work with Families*, London: Routledge and Kegan Paul.

Sainsbury, E. (1980), 'Client Need, Social Work Method and Agency Function', *Social Work Service*, 23.

Saltzberger-Wittenberg, I. (1970), *Psycho-Analytic Insight and Relationships: A Kleinian Approach*, London: Routledge and Kegan Paul.

Seligman, P. (1979), 'You Can't Win 'Em All' in D. Brandon and B. Jordan (1979).

Seve, L. (1978), *Man in Marxist Theory and the Psychology of Personality*, Brighton: Harvester Press.

Sharp, R. and Green, A. (1975), *Education and Social Control*, London: Routledge and Kegan Paul.

Sheldon, B. (1982), *Behaviour Modification*, London: Tavistock.

Siporin, M. (1975), *Introduction to Social Work Practice*, New York: Macmillan.

Specht, H. and Vickery, A. (eds) (1977), *Integrating Social Work Methods*, London, Allen and Unwin.

Spitzer, S. (1975), 'Towards a Marxian Theory of Deviance', *Social Problems*, vol.22, no.5, pp.638–51.

Stenson, K. and Gould, N. (1986), 'A Comment on "A Framework for Theory in Social Work" by Whittington and Holland', *Issues in Social Work Education*, vol.6, no.1.

Stevenson, L. (1974), *Seven Theories of Human Nature*, Oxford: Clarendon Press.

Stevenson, O. and Parsloe, P. (1978), *Social Service Teams: The Practitioner's View*, London: Department of Health and Social Services.

Stott, M. (1981), *Ageing for Beginners*, Oxford: Blackwell.

Timms, N. (1973), *The Receiving End*, London: Routledge and Kegan Paul.

Tinker, A. (1981), *The Elderly in Modern Society*, London: Longman.

Truax, C.B. and Carkhuff, R.R. (1967), *Towards Effective Counselling and Psychotherapy*, Chicago: Aldine.

Ullman, L.P. and Krasner, L. (1969), *A Psychological Approach to Abnormal Behaviour*, New York: Prentice-Hall.

Vevers, P. (1981), 'Bringing Up Baby', *Community Care*, 26 March, pp.12−13.

Walker, H. and Beaumont, B. (1981), *Probation Work: Critical Theory and Socialist Practice*, Oxford: Blackwell.

Watson, J.B. and Raynor, R. (1920), 'Conditional Emotional Responses', *Journal of Experimental Psychology*, no.3.

Webb, D. (1985), 'Social Work and Critical Consciousness: Rebuilding Orthodoxy', *Issues in Social Work Education*, vol.5, no.2.

Whittaker, J.K. (1974), *Social Treatment: An Approach to Interpersonal Helping*, Chicago: Aldine.

Whittington, C. and Holland, R. (1985), 'A Framework for Theory in Social Work', *Issues in Social Work Education*, vol.5, no.1.

Wilkes, R. (1981), *Social Work with Undervalued Groups*, London: Tavistock.

Williams, R. (1965), *The Long Revolution*, Harmondsworth: Penguin.

Wright Mills, C. (1963), *The Marxists*, Harmondsworth: Pelican.

Yelloly, M. (1980), *Social Work Theory and Psychoanalysis*, Wokingham: Van Nostrand Reinhold.

# Subject Index

# Name Index